DO ONE THING DIFFERENT

DO ONE THING DIFFERENT

And Other Uncommonly Sensible Solutions to Life's Persistent Problems

BILL O'HANLON

WILLIAM MORROW AND COMPANY, INC.
New York

It is the policy of William Morrow and Company, Inc., and its imprints and affiliates, recognizing the importance of preserving what has been written, to print the books we publish on acid-free paper, and we exert our best efforts to that end.

Library of Congress Cataloging-in-Publication Data

O'Hanlon, William Hudson.
Do one thing different : and other uncommonly sensible solutions to life's persistent problems / Bill O'Hanlon.
p. cm.
Includes bibliographical references and index.
ISBN 0-688-16499-4
1. Problem solving. 2. Insight. 3. Self-management (Psychology) 4. Solution-oriented therapy. I. Title.
BF449.043 1999
158.1—dc21 99-21578
CIP

Printed in the United States of America

First Edition

1 2 3 4 5 6 7 8 9 10

Book design by Michael Mendelsohn at MM Design 2000, Inc.

www.williammorrow.com

To Steffanie,
who helped me get used to the dark.
Once my eyes adjusted,
I could see lots of possibilities.

CONTENTS

ACKNOWLEDGMENTS

Thanks to Steffanie O'Hanlon, Loretta Barrett, and Darlene Hilton for comments and corrections. To Toni Sciarra for support and solid editorial guidance. To Bill Smythe for helping me to challenge insanity at the body level and to Lee Cartwright for helping me challenge insanity at the neurological level. To Annie Sprinkle, Susie Bright, Owen Morgan, and Betty Dodson, my mentors in doing one thing different in the area of sexuality. To David Whyte, for inspiration and guidance in the spiritual realm.

DO ONE THING DIFFERENT

CHAPTER 1

ANALYSIS PARALYSIS:

From Liabilities to Possibilities

> Socrates said the unexamined life is not worth living. But the (over)examined life makes you wish you were dead. Given the alternative, I'd rather be living.
>
> —Saul Bellow

There's an old story about a cop who comes upon a drunk crawling around talking to himself under a streetlight. The cop asks the drunk what he's doing, and the drunk answers in a slurred voice, "I dropped the keys to my house." The cop helps him look around. But after fifteen minutes, when there is still no sign of the keys, the cop suggests, "Let's retrace your steps. Where was the last place you remember having your keys?" "Oh, that's easy," replies the drunk, "I dropped them across the street." "You did!" cries the astonished cop, "Well, then why are we looking over here?" "There's more light here," replies the drunk.

In a similar way, when we have a problem, we often use the light of psychology and psychiatry to look for the key to solving it. Unfortunately, they do not always provide help. Instead, they have us, like the drunk, looking in the wrong place. Explanations often give us an illusion of help by enabling us to understand why we have a problem but not giving us any concrete ways to actually solve it. These systems of explanation can lead to a "victim culture," in which people focus on damage done to them in childhood or in their current relationships. This results in a tendency to blame others and look outside ourselves for solutions—to turn to experts or self-help books and groups.

Explanations are a booby prize. When you've got a problem, you want a solution. Psychological explanations, so pervasive in our society, steer people away from solving problems by giving them reasons why the problem has come about or why it is not solvable:

> "Jimmy has low self-esteem; that's why he is so angry."
>
> "I'm so shy that I'll never meet anyone."
>
> "I was sexually abused, so my sex life is bad."
>
> "She has dyslexia—that's why she can't read or write well."

One of my favorite illustrations of this problem of paralysis from overanalysis is in the movie *Annie Hall.* Woody Allen plays Alvey Singer, a neurotic (surprise, surprise). Soon after they meet, Alvey tells his girlfriend Annie that he has been in analysis for thirteen years. He is still clearly a mass of problems. When Annie Hall expresses amazement at how long Alvey has been in therapy without getting any better, he tells her that he knows this, that he intends to give it fifteen years, and that if he has not gotten any results by then, he's going to visit Lourdes.

Psychiatry, too, focuses on explanations, but its explanations are biological or genetic. Psychiatric theory—and theory it is—maintains that people's problems are based on biochemistry or even determined by biochemistry or genetics. But although we are born with and influenced by genetic and biochemical factors, not everything about us is determined by these factors. It's more complicated than that. People with biochemical problems can and do have fluctuations in their functioning and sometimes recover altogether from what seems like a neurological or biochemical disorder.

The problem with psychology and psychiatry as strategies for solving problems is that:

- They give you explanations instead of solutions.
- They orient you toward what can't be changed: the past or personality characteristics.
- They encourage you to view yourself as a victim of your childhood, your biology or genetics, your family, or societal oppression.
- They sometimes create new problems you didn't know you had before you came into contact with a program or a book.

Some people with dyslexia grow up to be successful writers. Some shy people become actors or public speakers. Some abused people have fine sex lives. They haven't let psychology, or ideas about what is wrong with them, dictate the course of their lives. They've taken a solution-oriented approach to life, focusing instead on what they can do to improve the situation.

I came to the solution-oriented approach by a very personal route. In 1971, I decided to kill myself. Now, this may seem like a strange introduction for a book designed to inspire you, but that's where it all began for me. I was very depressed and lonely at the time. I saw no possibilities for the future, aside from a continuation of the misery of the past. I considered myself a "poet" and certainly didn't want to work for a living. I was disillusioned by the hypocrisy I saw in society and in the people I knew. I felt as if I were all exposed nerves, as if I had no skin to protect me from the pain of the world or from contact with others. I was afraid to show my poetry to anyone but my close friends, so it wasn't likely that I would ever make a living as a poet. After a long, miserable time, I'd finally decided that I'd kill myself.

I was a hippie then, and the few friends I went to say good-bye to (who were generally as weird and depressed as I was) understood and accepted my decision. They would see me in another life, another trip around the wheel. It was too bad that things hadn't worked out for me in this life.

One of my friends, however, was very upset when she heard my plans for suicide. When I told her that the problem was that I just couldn't handle dealing with people and earning a living, she told me that she had some maiden aunts who would leave her some farmland in Nebraska when they died. She promised that I could live in a farmhouse on her land rent-free the rest of my life, if I would promise not to kill myself. Now, *that* seemed like a possibility to me. "How old are your aunts?" I asked. When I heard that they were in their sixties, I agreed not to kill myself. (I was young enough to assume that anyone in their sixties was bound to die soon. Little did I know that these maiden aunts in Nebraska routinely live to be 100!)

Now I had a future I could live for, but the challenge was figuring out how to live and be less miserable in the meantime.

I began searching for some way to feel better and have more of the things I wanted from life. I started reading psychology and self-help books. To my dismay, the more I read, the more depressed and discouraged I became. I began to realize how messed up I really was. I was "clinically depressed," and most probably I had a biochemically based brain disorder. I probably needed medications. Since I had been sexually abused when I was a child, the books indicated that a minimum of several years' worth of therapy was in order. I would have to spend lots of time, money, and energy getting in touch with the repressed, dissociated memories and feelings associated with the abuse. But I wasn't certain that I wanted to take medications or go through years of painful therapy. I was certain I couldn't afford either. No wonder I became even more depressed!

I have degrees in psychology and marriage and family therapy. But these approaches did not really show me how to help people (or myself) change. Most often, they led to interesting explanations of how a problem had developed and what kept it from changing. I began to search in a different direction. As I began to discover, the way to change was both simpler and less obvious than what I had learned. I eventually stopped looking in the obvious places (where there was more light) and focused my light on other areas to find the keys to solving problems. I found that other people were searching in these unorthodox places as well, and I learned all I could about what they had found that would help people change quickly and easily.

In my situation, analyzing why I was depressed was clearly part and parcel of the problem. Like the drunk under the streetlight, I was searching in all the wrong places for the key to let myself out of the prison that depression had become.

I spent those years studying, learning, and feeling steadily better. As it turned out, those aunts did live for many more years. I never got to take my friend up on her side of the bargain, because by the time she inherited the farmland I was already happy and successful.

I now have a great marriage, a successful career doing something I love, and a good income. I travel around the world teaching people the solution-oriented approach. You are holding my seventeenth book in your hands. (Finally, I was able to show someone my writing.) Much of what I discovered on my journey from misery and suicidal depression to happiness and success is encapsulated in this book.

One of the people who inspired me to develop the solution-oriented approach was a teacher of mine, the late psychiatrist Milton

Erickson. Erickson grew up on a farm in the Midwest and was much too pragmatic to get caught up in psychological or psychiatric explanations. When I studied with him in the late 1970s, he told me a story that illustrates the basic idea of the solution-oriented approach.

A favorite aunt of one of Erickson's colleagues was living in Milwaukee and had become quite seriously depressed. When Erickson gave a lecture there, the colleague asked him to visit the aunt and see if he could help her. The woman had inherited a fortune and lived in the family mansion. But she lived all alone, never having married, and by now had lost most of her close relatives. She was in her sixties and had medical problems that put her in a wheelchair and severely curtailed her social activities. She had begun to hint to her nephew that she was thinking of suicide.

After Erickson finished his lecture, he took a taxi to the aunt's house. She was expecting him, having been told by her nephew that he was coming. She met Erickson at the door and gave him a tour of the large house. She had had the house remodeled to allow wheelchair access, but other than that, it appeared as if nothing had been changed since the 1890s. The furniture and household decorations showed a faded glory, smelling of must. Erickson was struck by the fact that all the curtains were kept closed, making the house a depressing place indeed. The aunt saved the very best for last, however, and finally ushered Erickson into the greenhouse nursery attached to the house. This was her pride and joy; she had a green thumb and spent many happy hours working with the plants. She proudly showed him her latest project—taking cuttings from her African violets and starting new plants.

In the discussion that followed, Erickson found out that the woman was very isolated. She had previously been quite active in her local church, but since her confinement to a wheelchair she attended church only on Sundays. Because there was no wheelchair access to the church, she hired her handyman to give her a ride to church and lift her into the building after services had started, so she wouldn't disrupt the flow of foot traffic into the church. She also left before services had ended, again so she wouldn't block traffic.

After hearing her story, Erickson told her that her nephew was worried about how depressed she had become. She admitted that it had become quite serious. But Erickson told her that he thought depression was not really the problem. It was clear to him that her problem was that she was not being a very good Christian. She was taken aback by this and began to bristle, until he explained.

"Here you are with all this money, time on your hands, and a green thumb. And it's all going to waste. What I recommend is that you get a copy of your church membership list and then look in the latest church bulletin. You'll find announcements of births, illnesses, graduations, engagements, and marriages in there—all the happy and sad events in the life of people in the congregation. Make a number of African violet cuttings and get them well established. Then repot them in gift pots and have your handyman drive you to the homes of people who are affected by these happy or sad events. Bring them a plant and your congratulations or condolences and comfort, whichever is appropriate to the situation."

Hearing this, the woman agreed that perhaps she had fallen down in her Christian duty and agreed to do more.

Twenty years later, as I was sitting in Erickson's office, he pulled out one of his scrapbooks and showed me an article from the *Milwaukee Journal* (or whatever the local paper was called). It was a feature article with a large headline that read "African Violet Queen of Milwaukee Dies, Mourned by Thousands." The article detailed the life of this incredibly caring woman who had become famous for her trademark flowers and her charitable work with people in the community for the ten years preceding her death.

This book will give you ten keys to the effective new approach I discovered on my search: the solution-oriented approach to solving problems. These keys will translate the psychotherapy methods I use in my practice into simple, practical methods that you can use to solve your problems or just to make your life better and happier. You may use just one key or several. Potentially, any key could work for you; but in the solution-oriented approach, we believe that there are different solutions for different people and the only way to know which is right for you is to try them out and see.

I remember the first time I used the solution-oriented approach in my psychotherapy work.

I had just started working in a mental health center when a former client of another therapist sought help in an emergency. Janine's therapist, Louise, was on vacation and I had time available, so I agreed to see her for a session or two until Louise returned from out of town. Not wanting to interfere with what Louise would be doing when she returned, I thought I'd just ask Janine about her situation and not try to do any therapy.

Janine told me that she had sought therapy a year or so before for a serious episode of depression and that Louise had helped her come through that episode. She said that when she first saw Louise, she was so depressed that she was sleeping eighteen hours a day. She had been attending college on a scholarship, but when she became depressed she stopped attending classes, so she had failed all her courses and lost her financial support. This depressed her further, so now she had financial as well as emotional problems.

One day, in desperation, she called the local mental health center where Louise and I worked. Just getting out of bed and out of the house to come to see Louise lifted the depression a bit. But Louise could not see Janine more than once a week, as the mental health center had many clients to serve and her practice was full. Janine would hold on, waiting for the day she would see Louise, which always seemed to be a better day. Finally, the two of them had come up with the idea that just getting out of bed and getting out of the house would be helpful. But Janine had no money and had drifted away from her friends, so she had nowhere to go. They finally decided that Janine should get out of bed and take a walk around the block every day. At first, Janine found this nearly impossible. She had such low energy that it took an immense effort to get herself out of bed, put on some clothes, and drag herself around the block. But she did it. And she found that, amazingly, when she returned home from the walk she seemed to have more energy. So she started increasing her walk to two times, then three, and so on, until she was regularly walking five times around the block each morning.

As her mood began to improve, Janine began to contact friends from college. She started going out socially. On her walks, she bought a newspaper each day, and she starting applying for jobs until she found a part-time position. The next semester, she began attending classes part time as well. After a while, she had little or nothing to talk about during her sessions with Louise. They decided that the therapy was over.

What had happened recently, I asked, to make her depressed again? She said that she had met a man in one of her classes and they had gotten romantically involved. He had moved in with her. At first, things were fine; but after a time, he had become rather critical and controlling. He didn't like her friends, so she had stopped doing much socially with them. He had criticized her recent weight gain. He didn't like the way she chewed her food. They began to argue over everything. Finally, after a big fight, he threatened to move out, and she told him that would be fine with her.

For a few weeks, she felt fine. It was a relief not to be criticized and controlled. But then she plunged into a depression much like the previous one. She told me she was staying in bed a lot, sleeping. She had been calling in sick instead of going to work, and she was skipping some of her classes. As she described this to me, she suddenly stopped herself. "Wait a minute! I know what I need to do. I need to get out of bed and walk around the block, call my old friends, make sure I attend classes, and get to work. Wow, how could

I have forgotten that stuff?" She was smiling now—a contrast to the worried expression she had worn upon entering my office. "I know exactly what to do not to be depressed!"

"It certainly sounds like it," I replied.

When Janine left, I was excited. But I was also perplexed, because I hadn't done my usual therapist bit. I hadn't tried to solve Janine's problem, because I knew that Louise was going to return. And that turned out to be the key: *I* didn't solve Janine's problem—*she* did!

I had stumbled on *solution-oriented therapy*. Janine had used her own almost-forgotten solutions to solve her problem. I had helped her focus on what she did well and how she had solved problems in the past. Problem-oriented and explanation-based theories focus on what is wrong with a person or what went wrong in the past. Solution-oriented therapy highlights what is right with the person, what has worked or been helpful in the past, and what the person can do right now to change things.

Now, obviously, not everyone's depression can be solved quite so quickly and easily, but something important had happened here. According to psychological and psychiatric theories, such a rapid change could never happen in a case of severe depression. Obviously, that was wrong. Even people who are going to be depressed on and off throughout their lives can use this approach. If they have some tools that they can use to help them lessen or end a depressive cycle, they will be less hopeless and less depressed about their depression.

Don't get me wrong. I'm not trying to sell you the idea that anyone can get over a serious depression in twenty minutes. Most people would find it close to impossible even to struggle out of bed during the worst of a depressive episode. The point of Janine's story is that previously she had been able to get out of bed and walk around the block during the worst of her depression. And that is the essence of solution-oriented therapy: to find what people are capable of and what solutions they have previously used—and then get them to deliberately do the things they have found will work to alleviate or solve the problem. One person may have found reading an inspirational book helpful in the midst of a depression; someone else may have benefited from watching Marx Brothers movies while bedridden with a physical illness. These solutions wouldn't involve getting out of bed and walking around the block. Janine's solution came from Janine, not from me or from any psychological theory.

Earlier, I had learned the traditional therapeutic approach to helping people solve problems: find out what in their past has traumatized them and help them work through that trauma; or discover their irrational ways of thinking and help them correct that faulty thinking; or, perhaps, find a defect of biochemistry, in which case medications might help or they can be supported in accepting their situation.

Solution-oriented therapy is different: while taking into account that people might have a wide variety of problems—including biochemical, personality, or thought disorders or traumas from the past—it focuses on discovering what people are doing that works and helps them deliberately use that knowledge to eliminate problems. It encourages people to move out of analyzing the nature of the problem and how it arose and instead to begin to find solutions and take action to solve it.

What is so great about the solution-oriented approach is that, since it uses your solutions, you can act as your own consultant, and the remedies you find will be custom-tailored, so that they fit much better than remedies from some outside expert. You have the keys; you just need to know where to shine your light.

PART 1

CHANGING THE DOING OF THE PROBLEM

Insanity Is Doing the Same Thing Over and Over Again and Expecting Different Results

In this part of the book, you will learn to do something different when you are not happy or are not getting the results you want. This section focuses on concrete actions you can take to make changes. It shows you how to make changes by doing two things:

1. Pay attention to repetitive patterns you are caught up in or that others are caught up in with you, and change anything you can about those patterns.
2. Notice what you are doing when things are going better, and do more of that.

CHAPTER 2

WHEN LIFE HAS BECOME THE SAME DAMN THING OVER AND OVER AGAIN

Changing Patterns

When you discover you are riding a dead horse, the best strategy is to dismount.

—Dakota tribal saying

Get ready to learn a radically different way to approach life and solve your problems. At first, this approach may seem unbelievably simple. *My problems are more complicated and deeper-rooted than that*, you might think. But give this approach a chance. When you try it, you will discover the power of the solution-oriented approach. In recent years, this approach has been sweeping the field of psychotherapy. Most therapists had the idea that it takes years to make a significant change, especially with serious, long-standing problems. The solution-oriented approach has shown that people can make changes rapidly. I, and others who work this way, have taught thousands of therapists to approach problems in a solution-oriented way. Once therapists discover this way of working, they rarely go back to the old way.

The solution-oriented approach focuses on the present and the future and encourages people to take action and change their viewpoint. The past is important in the sense that it has influenced us and has brought us to where we are today, but letting it determine your future is a mistake. Instead, this approach suggests acknowledging the past and then getting on with changing things.

Some time ago, I read a letter to American advice columnist Ann Landers, one of the world's leading "therapists," that serves as a perfect introduction to this approach. A woman wrote telling other women not to complain if their husbands snore. For years her husband had snored ("like an elk") and she had always complained to him about it. He did not believe that he snored, so finally one night she told him she would prove it by setting up a tape recorder to capture the awful noise. She told him to go to sleep and snore to his heart's content. To her surprise, he did not snore loudly, but softly ("like a mouse"), that night. He never again snored loudly. Her letter ended poignantly: she noted that her husband had died a year before and that she missed him terribly and wished she could hear him snore like an elk again (Ann Landers column, *Omaha World Herald*, Sunday, December 13, 1987). How could the introduction of a tape recorder cure snoring? The answer is that when we keep doing the same thing over and over again, we get the same result. But if we do something different, change usually happens. Consider the following story:

> A man was imprisoned for years in China. One day in the shop where he worked in the prison, his eye caught little bits of bright wire amidst the shavings on the floor. He began gathering them and saving them in a bottle in his room to brighten things up a bit in the cell. After years of confinement, he was finally released from prison and brought the

> bottle full of wires with him to remind him of his years there. Now an old man and unable to work, he spent days waking at the exact hour the warden had decreed the prisoners should awaken and going to sleep at the usual prison lights-out time. He paced back and forth in his rooms in the same patterns he had while confined to his cell, four steps forward and four steps back. After some time of this, he grew frustrated one day and smashed the bottle. He found the mass of rusted wires stuck together in the shape of a bottle (Bette Bao Lord, 1990, p. 3).

When we have problems, most of us are like the man with his life in the shape of a bottle: we repeat the same actions over and over again and wonder why we get the same results. It's a bit like the stereotypical American tourist overseas trying to get directions from someone who speaks no English. When his question is not understood, he repeats it louder and slower: I . . . SAID . . . CAN . . . YOU . . . TELL . . . ME . . . HOW . . . TO . . . GET . . . TO . . . THE . . . EIFFEL . . . TOWER!

When what we are doing doesn't work, we often try it again, only this time louder or harder. Sometimes this persistence yields results (as any weary parent who gives in to the relentless pestering of a child can tell you), but more often it keeps us from getting what we want.

One way to solve a problem, then, is not to analyze why the problem arose, but to change what you are doing to solve it. The way to do that is to determine how you keep acting in the same way over and over again (the problem pattern) and begin to experiment with doing something different (breaking the pattern). This can even work when the problem is another person, for if you change your part of an interpersonal pattern, the other person will often change as a result of your change.

I call this changing the *"doing" of the problem*. This is what we will talk about in Part 1. In Part 2, we will take up changing how you see things as a way of changing the problem: I call that changing the *"viewing" of the problem.*

Solution Key 1:

BREAKING PROBLEM PATTERNS

A couple were seeing a marriage counselor because they couldn't seem to stop fighting. They would get angry with each other and let loose with the worst, most hurtful things they could say. Once something hurtful was said, they couldn't take it back, even though they regretted it when they calmed down. The counselor was exploring how both partners had learned this pattern from their parents; but although they now had some understanding of where the problem originated, the fights kept occurring.

The counselor attended one of my workshops and later told me what happened when he next saw this couple. The counselor told them that he had just been to a workshop and had learned something new. If they were game, they might want to try it. He couldn't vouch for its effectiveness, since it wasn't the way he usually worked; but he thought that in their situation, it might be just the thing they needed. They were willing to try anything, as the marriage was on the verge of being damaged beyond repair.

The counselor suggested that the next time they began an argument that seemed to be getting out of control, they should take a brief break and then meet in the bathroom. The husband should take off all his clothes and lie down in the bathtub. The wife was to stay fully clothed and take a seat next to the bathtub on the toilet. They were then to continue the argument where they had left off.

As you might imagine, it was difficult to have an argument that way. The husband felt absurd and exposed and wasn't his usual self.

The wife thought it was hilarious and couldn't quite work up her usual head of steam. But, as the counselor had suggested, for the next several weeks they dutifully performed this task each time they had an argument. After a few times of heading for the bathroom, however, they learned to modulate an argument so that it never went out of control. When things would start to get heated, one of them would glance toward the bathroom and the other would say, "Okay, okay, let's just calm down and see if we can talk this out."

Whenever you are stuck with a problem, try something new. Do something—just one thing—different. Break the pattern of the problem. *Insanity is doing the same thing over and over again and expecting different results!*

My friend Chris used pattern breaking with great success. She had two young children, and she found herself getting less sleep than she wanted. Chris wasn't a morning person, and she began waking up grouchy every morning, snapping at the children and her husband.

One day, her husband looked at her after she had blown up at one of the children for dawdling and asked, "What's wrong with you? Did you get up on the wrong side of the bed this morning?" She responded by snapping at him, but after the family had all left for work and school, she found herself taking the question seriously. Perhaps she had gotten up on the wrong side of the bed. The next morning, she would try changing her problem pattern.

So, the next morning, when it was time to get up, she rolled over to her husband's side of the bed (he was already in the shower) and climbed out. To her delight, the morning went entirely differently. She was not irritable. She kept getting up this way, and the good results lasted for quite a while—until one day she found herself getting cranky in the morning again. She found that she could again make a change, this time by crawling off the foot of the bed.

To repeat: this may seem unbelievably easy, but the only way you are going to find out if it works is to try it yourself.

Traditional explanations tell us that feelings cause behavior, but solution-oriented thinking says that maybe new actions can create new feelings.

When I first came across this idea in the 1970s, I was living in Arizona, and I had developed an allergy to grass pollen. At that time, I read a book about an Australian named Alexander, who had developed a method (called the Alexander method) of working with physical problems to cure them without medicine. Alexander had made his living as an orator until he developed hoarseness. None of the many doctors he consulted was able to cure this disorder, and he finally had to abandon his career.

Determined to solve the problem on his own, he began to do research on the body. Finally, one day he studied himself in a mirror while he was attempting to give an oration. He noticed that as he began to speak, he tensed his neck in a particular way and assumed a certain posture. He deliberately relaxed his neck muscles and changed his posture—and immediately got his voice back.

As I was reading about this and thinking about patterns, I decided I had nothing to lose, so I would try it on my allergy. I would observe any related pattern and change any part of the pattern I could.

So I began observing what I did in relation to my allergic reaction. Usually the pattern would start with a tickling sensation inside my nose. Then I would tense the muscles of my face in anticipation of a sneeze. Then I would sneeze about twenty times in a row. My nose would begin to run, and my eyes and the corners of my mouth would begin to itch. I noticed that once I started to sneeze, I could barely think, so I decided to try to break the pattern before the sneezing began.

I found that if I deliberately relaxed my facial muscles instead of tensing them, I would not sneeze. It was very difficult at first. I really wanted to give in to the tickle and sneeze. It just about drove me crazy not to sneeze, but I resisted the urge. If I didn't sneeze, my nose wouldn't run and the pattern would be broken. I wouldn't get the itchy eyes and mouth. After a few minutes, the urge to sneeze would diminish and finally go away altogether.

I had to break the pattern many times the first few weeks, but after that, my allergy was gone. At that point, I became a believer in the power of pattern breaking.

In order to break a pattern, you are going to have to become an anthropologist in regard to your problem. You are really going to have to study it, taking good notes and making clear observations. Stay away from theories and explanations. Go for descriptions. Attend more to the *what* and *how* than the *why* of the situation.

Breaking Patterns, Method 1: Change the "Doing" of the Problem

One way to do this is to imagine teaching someone to "do" your problem. If Meryl Streep or Robert De Niro were playing you in a movie and had to learn how to reproduce your problem, what advice would you give? How should the performer dress? What time of day should the problem happen or be most likely to happen? What should the performer say and do to get it started? How should it be kept going?

You can even use this idea for "feeling" problems. How would you "do" depression if you were going to do it your way? I know this one very well, since I informally majored in depression when I first attended college. The first thing I would do if I were going to get depressed is to stay in bed as long and as often as I could. If I did get out of bed, I would try to sit in one place in the house and not move much. I would definitely avoid going for a walk or a run or getting any exercise. Anything that would make me breathe very hard or move my body vigorously could endanger my depression. I would also avoid seeing or spending time with others. Mostly I would stay alone, brooding on my past and my faults. If I absolutely had to have some social contact, I would try to limit it to one or two people. With those people, I would limit my range of activities or topics of conversation. I would usually talk to them about how depressed I was and compare myself with others, always losing by comparison. (That is, I would note that others were more healthy than I was or had happier lives than mine.) That would be a good recipe for depression, wouldn't it?

Obviously, one thing to do to change such a depression would be to stop doing anything that was part of the pattern of "doing" depression and start doing anything else, anything that might break the pattern.

You can do the same thing with anxiety: How do you "do" your anxiety? Or jealousy: How do you "do" jealousy? Or chronic and unproductive arguments with your spouse: If I were you, what would I do to make it likely that a fight would start in my marriage? How could I keep it going or make it worse?

Here are six questions to ask yourself in order to discover a problem pattern:

1. How often does the problem typically happen (once an hour, once a day, once a week)?
2. What is the usual timing (time of day, time of week, time of month, time of year) of the problem?

   Does the problem happen only on weekends? Only at night? Right after you arrive home from work?

3. How long does the problem typically last?
4. Where does the problem typically happen?

   In the living room? The kitchen? The bathroom? At work? While you are in your car?

5. What do you do when the problem is happening?

Do you pound the table? Leave the room? Call up a friend and vent? Avoid seeing or talking to others? Rush for food or a cup of coffee?

6. What do others who are around when the problem is happening usually do or say?

   Do they give advice? Blame you or someone else? Use certain phrases or voice tones?

Once you identify the patterns you keep doing over and over again that are part of your problem, ask yourself: What would be a noticeable change that involves something you can do and would be willing to do? Usually this involves changing actions, which may include altering one or more of these factors:

- When the problem usually happens.

  One couple used to get into an argument every evening just after the husband arrived home from work. They decided that they would delay any discussions until after he had taken a quick shower and changed out of his work clothes. They were able to use this time change to avoid getting into arguments.

- What you do right before the problem happens.

  In college, I suffered from terrible insomnia. As I was a psychology student, I spent a lot of time tossing and turning, wondering what the deep roots of this psychological problem were. One night, as I was reading before I turned out my lights, I read about how much caffeine was in each cola drink. There, sitting on the nightstand, was a sixteen-ounce bottle of cola, which I routinely drank before I turned out the lights to try to sleep. I didn't drink the cola that night, and I had an easier time going to sleep. I subsequently stopped drinking cola entirely and was never troubled with insomnia again.

- What you do right after the problem happens.

  I had a client who routinely pulled out hairs from her head. She was going partially bald, but couldn't seem to stop this compulsive behavior. She told me that after pulling the hair out, she chewed on the root before discarding it. I suggested that she immediately discard the hair after pulling it out, without chewing it. She was able to stop pulling her hair out because she found it unsatisfying to do so without chewing it.

- What other people do before, during, and after the problem (if you can get them to agree to cooperate in making some changes).

- What clothes you wear when the problem occurs.

  A woman consulted me to help her stop bingeing and vomiting (symptoms of bulimia). I suggested she stop before she binged and put on her favorite shoes, no matter where she was or what she felt like. She agreed to follow the suggestion and was able to stop bingeing. She said that taking the time to put on the shoes gave her time to think about what she was doing, rather than just doing it automatically and compulsively.

- Where in the house or in the outside world you experience the problem.

- How you move (or don't move) your body while you are doing or having the problem.

- Any other typical actions or aspects of the problem situation.

  I once suggested to a woman who was bingeing and vomiting that she try bingeing on salad and learn to eat just a few chocolates (which she would normally never eat if she wasn't bingeing) slowly throughout the day.

Once I traveled to Argentina to teach a workshop on solution-oriented therapy. The participants wanted to see the approach demonstrated, so I asked for a volunteer from the audience: Did any audience members have a problem they were willing to discuss in front of the group, a problem they wanted to solve but hadn't been able to solve on their own? A woman came up to the stage and told me that she had gained a lot of weight recently and couldn't seem to lose it or to stop overeating. I told her that I wanted her to teach me how to gain or maintain weight, since I was finding that I was losing weight on my visit to Argentina. She told me that she always skipped breakfast. I told her that was my first mistake, since I almost always ate breakfast. Next, she would go to work, where someone always brought in some fattening pastries. She would vow to resist eating the pastries but would finally give in. She would then cut off the thinnest slice, vowing that it would be the only one she ate. But she would find herself returning to the pastries throughout the morning, each time taking only the smallest piece. Then, for lunch, since she had already made a pig of herself, she would eat only a salad with no dressing. She went without eating throughout the afternoon and then ate a regular dinner with her family at home. Then, late at night, after her children had gone to sleep and her husband had retired to the bedroom to read, she would stand at the freezer in the kitchen, compulsively eating ice cream.

We talked about where in the problem she could do something to break the pattern. She said she didn't really want to get up earlier in order to have time to eat breakfast, and she had already tried without success to resist the pastries. We finally settled on the ice cream. She agreed that if she felt the urge to eat ice cream, she would take it into the bedroom and eat it in front of her husband. Of course, she felt uncomfortable doing this and quickly cut out the compulsive ice cream eating. She began losing weight.

If you compulsively overeat cookies, one way to start to break the pattern would be to change the hand that you eat the cookies with. If you're right-handed, eat everything that is healthy and good for you with your right hand, but eat cookies and other problematic foods only with your left hand. Or try eating the cookies in the lobby of your apartment building instead of in your living room while you are watching television. Or dress up in your nicest outfit before you eat cookies.

If these ideas make you laugh, you are probably on the right track with regard to pattern breaking. Have fun with it. Be playful.

A family who came for therapy was constantly in conflict. The stepfather and stepdaughter were always arguing, and the mother felt caught in the middle. Both would try to get the mother to take their side, and she would try to keep the peace. The therapist suggested that the next time a typical argument began, the mother would stop the stepfather and stepdaughter, march them out to the backyard, and give them each a water pistol. They were to stand back to back without speaking as the mother counted off the paces for them. At ten paces, they were to turn and fire until their pistols were empty. The mother was to be the judge of who won this duel. As you might imagine, serious fun ensued and the arguments soon came down a notch, so that they could be resolved.

You can also link new things to the pattern, and that will sometimes break it.

A wife complained that her husband did not initiate sex or seem very interested in sex. She had talked to him a number of times about spicing up their sex life or increasing the frequency of sex, but he never seemed to follow through with his promise to initiate more. She was becoming more and more dissatisfied and often fantasized about having an affair with someone who was more passionate and more interested in sex. She had even started considering getting a divorce, since she didn't want to live the rest of her life without the passionate sex she longed for.

Finally, during an argument they were having in which he complained that she wasn't very consistent at doing the dishes, leaving them for him to do more often than not, she agreed to work on doing the dishes more often if he would agree to initiate sex after she had done a sinkful of dishes. She became much more diligent about doing the dishes, and he soon he become much more active in their sex life.

Jeff had a typical problem pattern. He would begin to brood about something that was bothering him about himself or about someone else. He would dwell on it and start to get anxious, a feeling he hated. He would begin to drink and withdraw from the people who were closest to him: his girlfriend, his parents, and his friends at work. He exercised regularly, but when he began to drink, he would stop exercising. After some days of this pattern, he would start to get very depressed and begin having panic attacks. This would bring him to his therapist.

The therapist, a solution-oriented practitioner, discussed the pattern with Jeff and they came up with some simple changes that interrupted the pattern. When he first noticed he was brooding on something, he agreed to talk to someone, usually his girlfriend, but it could be his parents, his friends, or even the therapist in a brief phone call. He also made a commitment that when he began to fell anxious, he would go exercise as soon as possible. This way, he never got to the part of the pattern in which he would drink and get panic attacks. He changed his problem pattern.

Don't do anything harmful, dangerous, illegal, or unethical

when you are changing your pattern. Otherwise, let your imagination run wild and get creative! Break out of your rut.

Summary of Method 1
CHANGE THE "DOING" OF THE PROBLEM

One way to change the pattern of the problem is to do something different when you have the problem. Pay attention to what you usually do when you have the problem and do it differently.

Breaking Patterns, Method 2: Use Paradox to Change the Problem Pattern

Many years ago, in Austria, this story circulated. A high school was putting on a play. One of the characters in the play stuttered. Since one of the students in that high school stuttered, the play's organizers decided they would invite him to play the part. It turned out that the young man who stuttered had always harbored a secret desire to be on the stage, and, with a little embarrassment and much excitement, he agreed. When he arrived for rehearsals, however, he discovered, to his amazement and chagrin, that he could not stutter when he deliberately tried to do so. His speech was clear and uninterrupted. The school finally had to find another student to play the part.

An Austrian psychiatrist, Viktor Frankl, heard this story and decided to apply it to his patients. He began to instruct patients with anxiety attacks to deliberately try to feel anxiety and panic. Of course, when they did, many of them had the same response as the stutterer in the example above—they couldn't.

Frankl went on to apply this technique, which he called *para-*

doxical intention, successfully to several other problems, mostly involving insomnia and impotence. He would instruct people who were trying to go to sleep to try to stay awake instead. Off to sleep they would go. He would instruct people who were trying to become sexually aroused to avoid getting aroused. The more they tried not to become aroused, the more aroused they would get. Frankl's idea was twofold: either people were interfering with the natural process of things by trying to control something that was automatic, or they were trying to stop something that was occurring naturally and the more they tried, the worse it got. So the solution was either to stop trying to solve the problem or to try to make the problem worse.

I was once consulted by a therapist who was having trouble helping one of his clients, a nineteen-year-old woman. She suffered from a unique form of agoraphobia (fear of going outdoors or leaving home). She was afraid of leaving home because she was convinced that she would have an "accident"—that is, that she would wet her pants if she couldn't get to a toilet quickly enough. She had arranged her life so she would always be within a short distance of a toilet. She did go out of the house at times. She could walk a route several blocks from her house to the community college she attended. She knew where each public toilet was on the way. She could also go for a ride with her mother, who agreed to drive only on approved routes, where the daughter had mapped out all the toilets along the way. At times during the trip, the daughter would panic and yell at her mother to stop immediately. She would run to the nearest toilet, sit down, and try to urinate. Of course, she would only be able to urinate a few drops at most, since she had been careful to urinate before leaving the house. She lived a limited life.

When I met her, I asked her if she had ever been surprised by something related to her problem. Had anything unexpected ever happened? She told me that her parents had divorced and she had chosen to live with her mother. Her father had come out better financially in the divorce than the mother, and both mother and daughter were upset with him because of this inequity. Also, the father wasn't very sympathetic about his daughter's problem, and he thought her mother was catering to her too much and thus making the problem worse. Still, the daughter tried to maintain a relationship with her father.

One day, the father asked his daughter out for lunch. She told him she would agree to go with him only if he agreed to drive on approved routes and stop immediately when she told him to. He agreed, but after picking her up, he pulled onto a freeway, deviating from the approved route. She began to panic and yelled at him to stop and let her out of the car. He refused and challenged her: "This is ridiculous! You are not going to wet your pants! I'll give you five hundred dollars right now if you can pee in my car." She was furious with him. He had a new car with a white interior. She really wanted to urinate in his brand-new car to pay him back for betraying her as well as to collect the money, which she and her mother could use. But as you might imagine, try as she might, she could not wet her pants. She finally calmed down when she realized that she wouldn't wet her pants, and they rode in silence to the restaurant.

This method is a bit like the advice given to people in movies who fall into quicksand. "Don't move," others say; "struggling only makes you sink. Relax and let yourself float. Then you can drift closer to the solid ground and pull yourself out." Instead of struggling against a problem by trying to solve it, go with it or relax and stop trying to make things better. This is usually a big change in "doing" and can get you out of being mired in the problem.

Summary of Method 2

USE PARADOX

One way to change the pattern of the problem is to try to make it worse (that is, more intense or more frequent). Or you can deliberately try to make the problem happen. Or just stop trying to avoid having the problem and instead embrace it and allow it to happen. This method works best for emotional or bodily problems like insomnia, anxiety, phobias, panic, and sexual arousal.

Breaking Patterns, Method 3: Link New Actions to the Problem Pattern

All life is an experiment. The more experiments you make, the better.

—Ralph Waldo Emerson

Another way to break a problem pattern is to link something else to the occurrence of the problem. It could be something that you think you ought to do but are not doing, or something that will help increase your motivation not to "do" the problem.

A woman who suffered from anorexia was now recovering. She wanted to maintain her weight, but as a substitute for eating, she had developed the habit of drinking water frequently throughout the day. Her problem now was that she still drank the water, so she would not realize she was hungry. She would forget to eat and would begin to lose weight again. With the help of a solution-oriented therapist, she decided to link having a glass of water to eating. Every time she had a glass of water, she ate some crackers and cheese, which she always carried with her. This way, she gradually worked herself back into the habit of eating and was able to keep her weight stable.

Alternatively, to help break the pattern, find something that is either burdensome or an ordeal and begin doing it every time you "do" the problem.

A couple came to me who were about to divorce. The problem, the wife said, was that the husband was a workaholic who stayed at work until late at night six days a week. On the seventh day, he would rest. That is, he would lounge in an easy chair all day and fall asleep watching television. The husband explained that his boss was taking advantage of him. He was a store manager on a training track to become a district manager of a chain of stores. The current district manager was trying to save money so he would look good at corporate headquarters, so he had convinced this man he couldn't hire the proper staff for his store. So the husband would have to stay late at the store stocking the shelves after finishing his regular tasks as a manager. He knew he should assert himself, but the boss was rather intimidating and threatened to prevent him from moving up the corporate ladder if he refused to go along.

The couple's pattern was very predictable. He would promise her that tonight would be different—he would try to be home early so they could spend the evening together. She would expect him home by dinnertime, around 6 P.M., but he would not arrive home until 10 or 11 P.M. Meanwhile, she would become so angry that when he did get home, they would get into a serious argument, lasting several hours, in which she complained and berated him and he defended himself and promised to mend his ways. As these fights became more frequent, he found more and more reasons to stay at work, hoping she would be asleep by the time he came home so that he would avoid a conflict. Recently, she had begun to go out to bars with her girlfriends several nights a week. He was quite upset about this, as he thought that going to bars with single friends was a setup for an affair. She was also calling friends and relatives long distance and running up quite a phone bill. She said that as long as he wasn't home, he had no right to complain—she had to do something to entertain herself.

After some discussion, I got them to agree to delay any action on their divorce proceedings and to try an experiment. Instead of stewing and getting upset, the wife should get an agreement from her husband about what time he would be home. They decided that seven o'clock was reasonable, giving him some leeway for unexpected delays and tasks. She should keep track of every minute after seven that he was late and "bank" the minutes. That is, she should not say a word to him about being late; instead, she should count the number of minutes he was late during the week. Then she could spend the same number of minutes doing one of three things: (1) She could spend guilt-free, hassle-free time at bars. (2) She could make that same number of minutes worth of long-distance phone calls, and he would not complain about the cost. (3) He would agree to spend the same number of minutes visiting either her parents or his parents on Sunday, again without complaint. This last was something she really enjoyed doing and he did only reluctantly, as Sunday was his only day off.

They tried the experiment and found that he came home by seven every evening, as he disliked the consequences so much that he wasn't willing to bring them on by being late.

Milton Erickson, one of my psychotherapy teachers, whom I mentioned earlier, told of a man who came to see him who had severe insomnia. This man hadn't been able to sleep well since his wife died a few years earlier. He would spend hours tossing and turning, trying to go to sleep. Finally, he would fall asleep at about four in the morning. In the past week, he had gotten only about twelve hours of good sleep. He lived with his son in a large house, and they shared the household chores. The man happened to mention to Erickson that he was glad his son lived with him because the house was filled with marvelous wooden floors that had to be waxed regularly, a task that he hated and that his son had agreed to do.

Erickson told the man that he could help him get over his insomnia but that it would require a commitment to work hard and make a great sacrifice. The man said he was willing to do whatever he needed to do, as this problem was driving him crazy and he had never been afraid to work hard. Erickson told the man that he was to go to bed at his regular time (around 8 P.M.). If he could still read the clock in fifteen minutes, he was to get up and wax the floors of the house until his normal wake-up time (6 A.M.).

After three exhausting nights, the man found that he still could not go to sleep on the fourth night in the required fifteen minutes and wearily got up and began waxing the floors. He soon became so tired that he couldn't continue. He decided to go rest his eyes for a few minutes in bed and then get up and continue. The next thing he knew, it was morning and he had gotten nine hours of sleep. He never again had a problem falling asleep. Erickson commented wryly that the man would do anything to get out of waxing those floors, even go to sleep!

In another variation of this "ordeal" method, Erickson advised a lawyer who suffered from insomnia to read the classics at night when he couldn't sleep. This man had worked his way through night school and always felt that his education was "second-rate" because he had never gotten around to reading great literature. He began falling asleep in his living room chair quite quickly every night, so Erickson advised him to stand up and lean against the mantel to read so he wouldn't fall asleep quite so quickly and could get more reading in. Eventually, this former insomniac became quite adept at falling asleep standing up.

You get the idea: Link some unpleasant activity to the occurrence of the problem. You'll probably find yourself getting over the problem very rapidly.

Summary of Method 3

LINK NEW ACTIONS TO THE PROBLEM PATTERN

Find something that you can do every time that you have the problem—something that will be good for you.

Find something that you think you should do but usually

avoid or put off. Every time you feel the urge to "do" the problem, do this avoided action first. If you aren't able to do that, do the avoided action for the same amount of time as the problem action, after the problem is over.

Make the problem an ordeal by linking it to something that you find unpleasant.

HOW TO BE SMARTER THAN A RAT

> The first rule of holes: When you are in one, stop digging.
>
> —Molly Ivins

There is a story about a man who went all over the world in search of wisdom. He wanted to know what made human beings tick and how the world worked. His search took him into many different disciplines. He studied spiritual disciplines, going from one religion to another. He studied martial arts, athletics, yoga, and other physical disciplines. Then he searched in academic disciplines: mathematics, physics, economics, geography, geology, sociology, and anthropology. Finally, he came to psychology.

By then, he had gathered some bits of wisdom about people and the world. But he had also figured out that there was a lot of speculation. He really wanted to cut to the heart of what psychology had to show him, so he could move on to the next area.

So he went to the library and looked for a book on psychology that he thought would be succinct and would contain the least speculation. He found a book that he thought would be just right for him. It was called *Things Psychology Has Proved*. (It was a fairly slim volume.) As he read it, he discovered that about all psychology had proved conclusively was that you can teach rats to run mazes and they will learn how to run the mazes faster and faster.

I did this as an undergraduate, so I learned how it goes. You take a white rat and put him at the beginning of a maze. There are four possible exits with a variety of removable slots, so you can vary the patterns of the maze.

To begin an experiment, you place some cheese at the end of one of the tunnels. Let's say you put it in tunnel 4.

You put the rat in the maze. Down the first tunnel he goes, and there's no exit and no food. The rat's hungry, so he goes to the second tunnel. No exit, no cheese. Third tunnel. No exit, no cheese. In the fourth tunnel, he finally finds the exit and finds the cheese. Pick up the rat, starve it some more to motivate it, put it at the beginning of the maze again, and place the food at the end of the fourth tunnel. The pattern repeats: First tunnel, second tunnel, third tunnel, no cheese. Finally the rat gets to the fourth tunnel again and finds his way out of this complicated maze and to the food. Pretty soon, you get a smart rat. When you put him at the beginning of the maze, he heads down the fourth tunnel and finds the cheese right away.

Now, you close tunnel 4. Then, cruel psychology student that you are, you test to see how long it takes for the rat to unlearn the old pattern and learn a new one. You open tunnel 2 and put the cheese there. You put the rat at the beginning of the maze. Right down the fourth tunnel he goes. No exit, no food. He retraces his steps, confused.

Back and forth the rat goes, and you record how many times he goes back and forth. Soon the rat gets really hungry and gives up going down the fourth tunnel. He goes down the first tunnel, then the second tunnel, and finds the cheese. If you keep putting the cheese at the second tunnel, the rat will begin consistently heading down the second tunnel.

The man reads all of this, closes the book on psychology, puts it back on the shelf, and thinks, "There's only a limited lesson that I can take from this in my quest for wisdom about people and how

Solution Key 1

BREAK PROBLEM PATTERNS

Method 1: **Change the "doing" of the problem**

To solve a problem or change things that are not going as well as you would like, change any part you can of your regularly repeated actions in the situation.

Method 2: **Use paradox**

Go with the problem or try to make it worse. Stop trying to fix the problem or make the situation better.

Method 3: **Link new actions to the problem pattern**

Add something new, usually something burdensome, to the situation, every time the problem occurs.

the world works. There's a big difference between rats and human beings. From what I've learned so far, if they get hungry, rats will eventually go down a different tunnel. But human beings will go down the same tunnel over and over again, thinking that the cheese will eventually be there. If it was there once, certainly it will be there again."

In my practice, I've noticed that sometimes people even take a chair and sit at the end of the fourth tunnel, waiting. They think, "I'll just hang out—I'm sure the cheese will be here soon." They think things like: *It was here in the family that I grew up in, so it's got to be here.* Or: *It was here in my last relationship, so I'm sure it will be here.* Or: *It makes sense that it should be here, so I'll just wait.*

All rats know is that they are hungry and they haven't yet found the cheese. On the other hand, human beings could *eat their beliefs* for decades. Using the solution-oriented approach, you can find the "cheese" in your life by making an end run around those beliefs and ideas you've gotten. Eventually, perhaps you can become smarter than a rat in regard to your problem.

For many people, Solution Key 1 is all they need to solve their problems, or at least to get off the dime and begin to make changes. Don't despair if this key hasn't worked for you. (You have used it, haven't you? It surely won't work if you don't even try it.) In Chapter 3, you will learn to use Solution Key 2: Find and Use Solution Patterns.

CHAPTER 3

BECOMING SOLUTION-ORIENTED

Doing What Works

Man only likes to count his troubles, but he does not count his joys.

—Fyodor Dostoyevsky, *Notes from the Underground*

One of the quickest ways to change patterns is to find something you already do that works. This is reminiscent of the "African violet queen of Milwaukee" in Chapter 1. Erickson saw her interest and skill in working with plants as a way to help overcome her isolation and depression. Where are the African violets in your life that you can use to change your patterns and solve your problems?

Solution Key 2

FIND AND USE SOLUTION PATTERNS

The next solution-oriented method of solving problems, then, is to find something you or someone else did that made a problem a bit less severe or solved it altogether. This is really a variation on the theme from Chapter 2. When what you are doing isn't working, do something else. One "something else" is to do something that worked previously. These previous solutions are easy to do (because you already know how to do them), and they fit into your natural environment, so they are not as alien as someone else's ideas or solutions—even good ideas or solutions—might be.

An easy and effective way to solve a problem is to find an example of a time when things went better in regard to the problem and start to deliberately put parts of actions you used at that time into the problem situation. Here are four areas to shine your light on.

Finding Solutions, Method 1: Ask Yourself: When Didn't I Experience the Problem After Expecting That I Would?

Most people can recall a time when they expected to have a problem, but for some reason it didn't happen. Recall such a time or incident.

Maybe you and your spouse were about to start your usual bickering, but somehow you avoided it. How do you explain why things went better? How did your partner respond when the problem didn't happen or didn't run its usual course? Did he or she begin joking, or soften his or her voice, or reach for you?

Was there ever a time when a usual problem started to occur but was interrupted or didn't really play itself out in the usual troublesome way? For example, can you recall a time when you would ordinarily have gotten scared about something and begun to avoid it, but somehow you developed more confidence and decided to go forward with it?

When you find such a time, think about what you did differently. If you usually eat a bag of cookies at night and don't like the resulting weight gain, think of a night when, for whatever reason, you didn't eat the cookies. The reason may have been that someone was visiting, that you had had a big lunch and weren't as hungry as usual, that you had some exciting news and weren't as tired as usual, or that you went on a diet. But the reason is not the focus here. The focus is on what action you took instead of overeating that night. Did you spend time reading, going to the movies, cleaning out a closet, talking to a friend on the phone? That action may be the key to solving the problem. In the solution-oriented approach, we suggest that, instead of analyzing why you were able to have a cookieless night, *you deliberately reproduce now what you did spontaneously then*. If, when you arrive home tired and are likely to eat cookies, you instead sit down and read, call a friend, go to the movies, or clean out the closet, you will find that you are much less likely to reach for the cookies. Instead of focusing on "why you do," focus on "what you do." Then take action. You don't have to be perfect at it or do it every night. Just begin to use your solution pattern and find out what happens. If you are like most people, you will discover that, by taking action that works, you will begin to *feel* different. You will not feel so stuck. You will most likely not feel so tired. And as you feel different, it will be easier to do something different.

Summary of Method 1

ASK YOURSELF: WHEN DIDN'T I EXPERIENCE THE PROBLEM AFTER EXPECTING THAT I WOULD?

Find a time that is an exception to the usual problem pattern and mine it for changes you can make in the situation by deliberately repeating whatever action worked.

Finding Solutions, Method 2: Notice What Happens as the Problem Ends or Starts to End

To decrease the frequency of a problem or to hasten its departure from your life, sometimes it is possible to use aspects of what happens as the problem subsides. Usually this involves discovering controllable *actions* that have spontaneously happened when the problem has ended or started to subside and making those actions more deliberate during future occurrences of the problem. This time, you do those actions much more quickly than usual—and you do them consciously, not accidentally.

A couple with whom I was doing marriage counseling had experienced times when there was a "cold war" between them. When things would get tense, they would first exchange words but then withdraw into silence for days at a time. I asked them how the cold started to thaw. They replied that one way things thawed was when they talked over the phone. One of them traveled frequently on business and even if they were in the midst of a difficult time, they always seemed to reconcile when they spoke over the phone. Perhaps it was the distance, or maybe they did better without the visual component. Whatever it was, they decided they would experiment with using the two phone lines in their house to call each other within an hour after a cold war started. They tried this and found that it often helped them thaw much more quickly.

Summary of Method 2

NOTICE WHAT HAPPENS AS THE PROBLEM ENDS OR STARTS TO END

Then deliberately do some of the helpful actions you do then, but do these actions much earlier in the problem situation.

Finding Solutions, Method 3: Import Some Solution Patterns from Other Situations in Which You Felt Competent

You can often find solutions by thinking of areas in your life that you feel good about, including hobbies, specialized knowledge, or well-developed skills. I call these *contexts of competence.* Is there anything you know or do in one of those areas that would be helpful in solving a problem you are facing? Perhaps you have developed great patience knitting sweaters that you can use to help you react more patiently to your teenager when he or she is trying your patience. Have you learned anything from your job in marketing, like listening to the customer's needs, that would help you get along with your spouse? Do you know something out on the golf course that you forget when you get behind the wheel of your car?

I was consulted by a woman who was unhappy with her marriage. Instead of seeking couples therapy, though, she had decided that she needed to do all the work herself. Her husband was "moody," she said; this turned out to mean that he would yell at her and call her names. He had previously been physically abusive and had stopped that, so she felt she couldn't ask him to make any more changes.

She said, "I think I just need to accept my husband the way he is. He's just moody. He can't change."

I said, "I'm not sure I agree with you. I think he can change his moodiness, just as he changed his violent behavior."

She said, "I don't think he can."

I objected. "Wait a minute. Your friend who referred you to me said that you were a really good horse trainer. She said you were so good with horses that she couldn't believe it. You were extraordinary."

She said, "Oh, yeah, I think I'm pretty good with horses."

I said, "Well, tell me, what would you do if somebody brought you a horse and said it was impossible to train? Just absolutely impossible to train."

She said, "There's no such thing as an impossible-to-train horse!" She sat up and had more strength in her voice.

I said, " What if someone told you that this horse was impossible to train?"

She said, "I wouldn't accept it. There is no such thing as an impossible-to-train horse."

I asked, "How would you go about training such a horse?"

She said, "Well, there are four simple principles for horse training."

"Four?" I took out my notepad and asked, "Okay, what are they?"

"The first one," she said, "is don't try and teach the horse more than one thing in each training session. Even if you think the horse has learned it in the first five minutes and the training session is an hour, don't try to teach the horse more than one thing. You'll just confuse the horse. Just go over that one lesson until you think the horse has learned it."

I wrote, "Go for small changes and once the horse has learned one thing, give it a rest."

"The second thing," she said, "is, if you get upset with the horse, you are not doing training anymore. You are punishing the horse. So if you get upset or hooked in, get off the horse, take a walk, come back later when you're fresh or come back the next day if you can't let it go that day. Then start again."

I wrote, "Don't get hooked or upset or you'll be punishing rather than training."

"The third thing," she said, "—and this is hard to explain if you don't ride horses—but sometimes I'm not mad at the horses, I'm not hooked in, but they are not cooperating. They are fighting me all the way. Here I am, this wiry little person, and these are racehorses. They're tough and they're strong and they are just not cooperating with me, so I'll just drop the reins. It's pretty scary because I've been thrown off horses and smashed into fences and stuff. But when I drop the reins, there is nothing to fight against. The horses calm down and then slowly, I pick up one of the reins, then the other one, and I reestablish that I'm in charge."

So I wrote, "Give up the small control to stay in charge."

"The fourth thing," she said, "is that once you have selected the approach you are going to use with the horse, stay with it. Don't change approaches. Be consistent, and the most difficult horse will come around."

I wrote, "Choose a consistent approach and stick with it."

I tore the page off my notepad and handed it to her, saying, "Here. Pretend your husband is a horse. I'm an expert on husbands, just as you're an expert on horses. I think your husband is trainable. As I say to my wife, 'I'm a slow learner but I'm trainable. Work with me here.' I think your husband is trainable. Just as you wouldn't accept that a horse is impossible to train, I don't accept that your husband is impossible to train."

For her, the lightbulb came on at that moment. She went home with a clear plan for how to "train" her husband to be more polite and less abusive.

Another way to identify contexts of competence is to think

about times when someone you know has faced a similar problem and resolved it in a way that you admired and would like to emulate. Perhaps you know someone who was fired from a job and handled it in a way you admired. Could you use any of what he or she did in that crisis as a model for how you handle things after finding out that your teenager is heavily into drugs? Or maybe you read a biography of someone who followed his or her dreams even when pressured by others to follow a more conventional course. Is there any part of this that you could use in facing up to your fear of flying?

Summary of Method 3

IMPORT SOME SOLUTION PATTERNS FROM OTHER SITUATIONS IN WHICH YOU FELT COMPETENT

Examine your patterns at work, in your hobbies, with friends, and in other contexts to find something that you can use effectively in the problem situation.

Finding Solutions, Method 4: Ask Yourself: Why Isn't the Problem Worse?

How do you explain the fact that your situation or problem isn't more severe than it is? This is a strange way of finding solution patterns, but it often works.

A man who often weighed as much as 280 pounds told me that his eating and weight were out of control. I asked him why he didn't weigh 350 pounds. He gave me a funny look but said he couldn't stand it if he weighed that much. I told him that I understood, but I still wasn't sure what he did to make sure he didn't gain that extra

70 pounds. He said that whenever he reached 280, he would begin to modify his eating (so he wasn't quite as out of control as he had said) and increase his exercise. Our strategy, then, was to get his patterns to change in the same way *before* he reached this peak weight. He already knew how to lose weight—he just wasn't using what he knew soon enough. Now, obviously he had to be motivated to make these changes, so we investigated what kinds of things motivated him. He would look at the scale, look at himself in the mirror, think of not being able to fit into his clothes, and begin to feel motivated. We agreed that he would practice these strategies when the scale showed 270 pounds instead of waiting for it to hit 280. In this way, we were able to use what he already did to help him gradually decrease his weight.

In the next example, you will see solution-oriented therapy used to help solve a serious problem. What seemed like a difficult, scary problem became much more manageable when solution strategies were used. When I first heard about this case, it seemed intimidating: here was a young man with a serious psychiatric problem who might be dangerous. But after I met him and we used solution-oriented methods, he seemed much more changeable and less threatening.

I consulted on a case in which a young man, married only a few years, had become convinced that the devil was visiting him every night and having anal sex with him. It had all started, Richard said, after their child was born and his wife started sleeping in the living room. She was a seamstress and would doze and work throughout the night, so she started to take catnaps in the living room. All alone in their bedroom, Richard was visited one night by a spirit, he told me, that had begun to perform oral sex on him. Because he and his wife had not had sex for some time, he was happy for the visitation, even though he felt a little guilty about betraying his wife with the spirit. The spirit began to visit quite regularly, but gradually became more and more violent with him, sometimes hurting his penis by biting and sucking it too hard. He started to resist, but alas, it was too late. The spirit had developed some sort of power over him and could do things to him even without his consent. He became frightened and went to the library one day to look up some information about spirits. He found that the spirit who was visiting him was probably a succubus, and that it came from the devil. He was very frightened when he learned this and sought the advice and help of his minister. The minister, a very wise and gentle man, reassured him that it was most probably a psychological and emotional issue related to his marital problems. He urged Richard to talk to his wife and sort out their difficulties. Richard did confess to his wife, who was concerned but also understanding. For a time, the nightly visits stopped and the couple began having sex on a more regular basis. But one night the wife was working on a project, and the spirit visited again—this time more malevolent and intrusive than ever. This time it began to penetrate Richard's anus with what felt like a burning hot penis. He resisted, but to no avail. Richard was raped anally that night and regularly in the nights that followed. The penis began to travel up his colon and wrapped itself around his heart. He became terrified that he would have a heart attack and began having trouble breathing during the attacks. He again sought out his minister and also talked to his wife and his parents. The minister, at the urging of Richard's parents (who were convinced this was a spiritual problem), found an exorcism prayer and said it for Richard. That relieved the situation for a little while. But now the wife's parents, whom she had informed, became involved. The in-laws were concerned for their daughter's safety and were convinced that Richard had psychological problems that should be treated by a psychiatrist. A struggle ensued between the two sets of parents and the couple, and soon the devil reappeared and the anal rapes began anew. Richard was afraid to have sex with his wife now, because he was afraid that the devil would enter his wife through him while they were having sex. Finally, to appease his wife (and her parents), he sought counseling.

Richard was fairly convinced that the devil was behind it all. But he had considered that it might be a psychological problem. He just wanted help and to have the attacks stop.

I told him that I was not certain what the nature of the problem was. It might be of supernatural origins or it might be something else. My job was to find out what could help. Through some discussion, we found that there were four things that seemed to diminish the likelihood of an attack:

1. Having sex with his wife. The minister had assured him that since God had sealed the bonds of his marriage, the devil could not enter into them while they were having sex. The minister had therefore recommended that the couple have sex as often as possible to keep the devil at bay. (See, he was very wise.) They had recently been following his advice, and it had helped.
2. Saying the exorcism prayer had helped for a little while.
3. Talking to his wife and the minister about the visits helped. After he did so, the devil wouldn't visit that night. I asked whether telling me might have the same effect, and he thought it might, since he felt less guilty and less frightened after he told me and I didn't criticize or coerce him. But talking with his parents or his in-laws was not helpful in the same way. In fact, when his parents and in-laws had become more involved, the visits were worse and more frequent.
4. One night he got up out of bed as he was being visited by the devil and ran down the street (with his clothes on). The devil hadn't seemed to be able to follow him and also didn't return that night.

Of course, we made a plan to increase the four activities that helped; and soon after, the devil's grip on the young man seemed to loosen. The couple jointly decided to put some more distance between them and their parents.

Was Richard's problem neurological and biochemical? I can see my psychiatrically, medically minded readers nodding their heads vigorously. And perhaps they are right. Could it have been spiritual in origin? I can see other readers thinking that I have finally hit the nail on the head. And I can see still others thinking that it was really a psychological or interpersonal problem.

But in the solution-oriented approach, we are not going to focus on what the problem really is—we focus just on what helps. It could have turned out that medication helped. It did turn out that prayer helped somewhat. It also helped that Richard become closer to his wife and put more distance between the couple and their parents. Lastly, running helped. Was that because of a change in brain chemicals, triggered by physical activity? Distraction? Getting out of the house? Who knows? Richard just knows that he is doing better and is not plagued by the devil any longer. That's good enough for him.

Richard did continue in therapy and, of course, had other things to work on. But he was now on the right track. I shudder to think of what his fate would have been had he gone the traditional route. He would probably now be a long-term psychiatric patient, resigned to taking only partially helpful medications (the devil might still visit, but less often), and he probably would be divorced from his wife.

Now, before the psychiatrists or the psychiatrically minded out there jump on me, I want to say that I think some people are helped greatly by modern psychiatric medications. And, of course, not everyone does well with a solution-oriented approach. But in Richard's case, it *did* work and saved him a lot of grief and future problems. If it can work in such a serious case, surely it's worth a try to see if it can help solve your problems.

Solution Key 2

FIND AND USE SOLUTION PATTERNS

Method 1: Ask yourself: When didn't I experience the problem after I expected I would?

Method 2: Notice what happens as the problem ends or starts to end. Then deliberately do some of the helpful actions you do then, but much earlier in the problem situation.

Method 3: Import some solution patterns from other situations in which you felt competent.

Method 4: Ask yourself: Why isn't the problem worse?

Summary of Method 4

ASK YOURSELF: WHY ISN'T THE PROBLEM WORSE?

Then use your own natural abilities to limit the severity of the problem you have been using without noticing.

In Chapter 2, we spoke about breaking up problem patterns. That is also what Solution Key 2 does, but it accomplishes this by steering you toward patterns that have already worked but that you haven't noticed you haven't been using regularly. Next, in Part 2, we'll take up another major element of the solution-oriented approach—changing how you think about and see your problems.

PART 2

CHANGING THE VIEWING OF THE PROBLEM

There's Nothing as Dangerous as an Idea When It's the Only One You Have

In this part of the book, we will focus on another solution-oriented approach: changing how you think and what you pay attention to as a way to change your situation for the better. This can involve five things:

1. Acknowledge your feelings and your past without letting them determine what you do.
2. Change what you are paying attention to in a problem situation.
3. Focus on what you want in the future rather than on what you don't like in the present or the past.
4. Challenge unhelpful beliefs about yourself and your situation.
5. Use a spiritual perspective to help you transcend your troubles and to draw on resources beyond your usual abilities.

CHAPTER 4

ACKNOWLEDGMENT AND POSSIBILITY

Getting Beyond the Past and Your Feelings

> To fear is one thing. To let fear grab you by the tail and swing you around is another.
>
> —Katherine Paterson

When we get stuck in life, often we begin to see things in the same way over and over again. We lose our creativity in the problem area. One way to regain creativity is to challenge the idea that your past or your feelings make you act in any specific way in the present. I call this *changing the "viewing" of the problem.* In this chapter, you'll learn an easy way to handle the past and your feelings.

We are often advised by psychological experts to "get in touch with our feelings" and to "go with them" or express them. What I suggest is that you first acknowledge your feelings and then decide whether or not it is a good idea to act on them or express them. Sometimes it is and sometimes it isn't. Sometimes it is actually better to ignore or transcend your feelings.

Long ago, in Tibet, there was a ceremony, held every hundred years, which Buddhist students could undergo in order to attain enlightenment. All the students would line up in their white robes. The lamas—the Tibetan priests—and the Dalai Lama would line up before the students. The Dalai Lama would begin the ceremony by saying, "This is the ceremony of the Room of 1,000 Demons. It is a ceremony for enlightenment, and it happens only once every hundred years. If you choose not to go through it now, you will have to wait another hundred years. To help you make this decision, we'll tell you what the ceremony involves.

"In order to enter the Room of 1,000 Demons, you just open the door and walk in. The Room of 1,000 Demons is not very big. Once you enter, the door will close behind you. There is no doorknob on the inside of the door. In order to get out, you will have to walk all the way through the room, find the door on the other side, open the door (which is unlocked), and come out. Then you will be enlightened.

"The room is called the Room of 1,000 Demons because there are one thousand demons in there. Those demons have the ability to take the form of your worst fears. As soon as you walk into the room, those demons show you your worst fears. If you have a fear of heights, when you walk into the room it will appear as if you are standing on a narrow ledge of a tall building. If you have a fear of spiders, you'll be surrounded by the most terrifying eight-legged creatures imaginable. Whatever your fears are, the demons take those images from your mind and seem to make them real. In fact, they'll be so compellingly real that it will be very difficult to remember that they're not.

"We can't come in and rescue you. That is part of the rules. If you go into the Room of 1,000 Demons, you must leave it on your own. Some people never leave. They go into the Room of 1,000 Demons and become paralyzed with fright. They stay trapped in the room until they die. If you want to take the risk of entering the room, that's fine. If you don't, if you want to go home, that's fine.

You don't *have* to enter the room. You can wait until you are incarnated again, come back in another hundred years, and try it again.

"If you want to enter the room, we have two hints for you. The first hint: As soon as you enter the Room of 1,000 Demons, remember that what they show you isn't real. It's all from your own mind. Don't buy into it; it's an illusion. Of course, most of the people who went into the room before you couldn't remember that. This idea is very difficult to keep in mind. The second hint has been more helpful for the people who made it out the other side and became enlightened. Once you go into the room, no matter what you see, no matter what you feel, no matter what you hear, no matter what you think, *keep your feet moving.* If you keep your feet moving, you will eventually get to the other side, find the door, and come out.

Solution Key 3

ACKNOWLEDGE YOUR FEELINGS AND THE PAST, WITHOUT LETTING THEM DETERMINE YOUR ACTIONS IN THE PRESENT OR THE FUTURE

This approach, you may have noticed, isn't big on the past. There haven't been any exercises or discussions about resolving your childhood trauma or admitting that you are an adult child of anything. The solution-oriented approach is focused primarily on the present and the future, because that is where change occurs. You may also have noticed that there hasn't been much focus on getting in touch with, working through, and expressing your feelings. This approach is much more focused on actions and points of view. You might be able to get your problems solved by rehashing the past and your feelings, but often that approach just leads to endless self-analysis.

But even though solution-oriented therapy focuses on changing the doing and viewing, and on the present and the future, this doesn't mean that you don't deal with the past or your feelings. You just keep them in their proper perspective.

Acknowledgment, Method 1: Acknowledge Your Own Experience, Feelings, and Self

We keep these elements of life in perspective by acknowledging them. Acknowledgment has great power. Years ago the psychologist Carl Rogers developed an entire method of therapy based on this powerful principle. Using this simple procedure could save you months of therapy. Merely acknowledge and accept as valid everything that goes on inside you and who you are. To acknowledge means to notice and allow whatever is there to be there. Instead of trying to get rid of it, hide it, analyze it, or judge it, just let it be. Rather than thinking you have to do something about it, just let yourself be aware of it. Whatever fantasies, thoughts, feelings, sensations, or perceptions you have, accept them as they are. You don't have to like them—just accept that that is what's happening for you at this time. Whoever you are at the core, just let yourself be that way.

There's an old saying in therapy that captures this principle well: You've got to be where you are to get where you are going. If you resist or deny where you are and who you are, it is hard to move on to where you want to be.

Imagine you are in a room filled with furniture. If you don't acknowledge where you are or if you fool yourself about where you are, you are going to run into a lot of unexpected obstacles and frustration trying to get out of that room. If you know where you are, you may still encounter obstacles, but you'll anticipate their location and takes steps to avoid them.

Another result of not acknowledging where you are is that you may get stuck with feelings or memories that would probably be transient if you didn't resist them or get down on yourself for having them.

Once a new client came to my office in great agitation. When I asked what his trouble was, the man replied earnestly and desperately, "I'm a latent homosexual!" I don't like this Freudian self-labeling stuff, so I told him just as earnestly, "You are a latent many things: a latent dog, a latent president of the United States. What makes you think you're gay?" The man reported that lately he had been having fantasies of nude men while he was having sex with his wife. These fantasies had grown in intensity until they dominated his attention during sex with his wife. He feared he was becoming a homosexual. I asked the man if he wanted to pursue a gay life. He adamantly maintained that he was seeking help because he did not want to act on these fantasies, although deep down he feared he would. I said that if he decided he was gay, I would help him come to terms with it, but that I had heard nothing to clearly indicate that he was.

The man was amazed. "What about these fantasies?" he asked. I explained that there is a difference between fantasy and action. Perhaps these fantasies were a message from deep inside about his real desires, but perhaps they were just random fantasies. I told him that I suspected that the fantasies had happened infrequently at first and that the more the man had tried to get rid of them, the more intense and frequent they became. He said that this was true. I recommended an experiment. Every time he started to make love with his wife, and even at random times during the day when he had a free moment, he should try to make the fantasies of nude men happen. A week of diligently practicing this exercise convinced the man that the more he encouraged the fantasies, the less they ran the show.

This story contrasts with that of another client, whose parents urged him to get help after they heard him speak seriously about killing himself. After several sessions, he very nervously and tentatively told me that he had been attracted to men for quite some time. I gave him my usual talk about accepting and acknowledging one's thoughts, feelings, and desires. In the next session he told me that he had gone home and thought a lot about what I'd said. It had become clear to him that although he had tried over the years to be attracted to women, he wasn't. He had been fearful that his family would not accept him if he was gay. The conflict had nearly driven him to suicide. We started to work on self-acceptance and how he would deal with his family and others. In the end, he decided that he would tell only selected family members who would be likely to take the news well. By the time others in his family found out, he was much more accepting of his sexual identity and thus better able to deal with their reactions. His suicidal impulses disappeared.

In both of these cases, the simple act of acknowledgment led to resolution. The power of acknowledgment extends to the body as well. Some years ago, I was teaching a class helping people get off the diet roller coaster. Part of my talk involved accepting one's body just as it is currently and not waiting to lose weight to feel okay about oneself. One participant said she knew what I was talking about. She had recently been paging through a scrapbook and had come across a picture of herself five years before. As she looked at it, she realized that she liked how she looked and how much she weighed at that time, which was about fifteen pounds less than she weighed currently. She was thinking that if she could only get back to that weight, she would feel good about her body. Then she remembered where and when the picture was taken and how terrible she had felt then about her body. In that moment she realized that it was more important to find self-acceptance where she was now—otherwise, she might look back five years from now and think the same thing about where she was now. Not accepting herself was a key element in her gaining more and more weight, as she would eat more in an attempt to alleviate her depression about her body.

I hope these examples show that there is great power in acknowledging and validating who you are and where you are, which includes the feelings, thoughts, perceptions, and body you currently have.

Summary of Method 1

ACKNOWLEDGE YOUR OWN EXPERIENCE, FEELINGS, AND SELF

This means accepting what you are feeling, sensing, and thinking, as well as your body and who you are, without judgment.

Acknowledgment, Method 2: Acknowledge Others' Feelings and Points of View

One of the most frequent complaints I hear while doing therapy with couples is: "You aren't hearing me." This introduces another aspect of the power of acknowledgment: acknowledging others' experiences and their own sense of themselves.

A lot of relationship problems are rooted in the game "who's right, who's wrong." Couples spend their time and energy arguing about who is right and who is wrong instead of working together to solve whatever problem they are facing. A good way to bypass these problems is to distinguish between private truth and public facts. Your private truth is what goes on inside you, what I call your experience and your sense of yourself. It's private because no one can know about it unless you somehow let people know about it, through words or actions. So, a good rule of thumb is to avoid arguments about whether someone else's private truth (perceptions, feelings, thoughts, and so on) is right or wrong. Just acknowledge the other person's private truth. You might say something like, "You thought I was criticizing you when I said I was lonely," or "You wanted me to call and were angry that I didn't." You are not agreeing with the other, or saying that he has a monopoly on the truth—you are saying only that he feels and perceives things a certain way and that you hear him and understand that he has a right to that experience.

Public facts are another matter. They are based on observation: what you and others can observe with the senses of sight, taste, smell, sound, and touch. In this area, you can argue about who is right or wrong. (We'll discuss this aspect of relationships in more detail in Chapter 9.)

I recommend acknowledging rather than trying to judge, change, or analyze another person's core self. Once, as I was working with a couple in therapy, the man suddenly became agitated and said to his wife and me, "You two are trying to change me, and I won't change!" Now, I happened to like this guy, even though he could be quite obnoxious. So, I said, "No, I find you obnoxiously charming and wouldn't ever want to change that. All we're discussing here is getting you to talk differently and do different things with your wife so that the relationship works better for the two of you. I'm not trying to change who you are; I'm just trying to change a few things you do." With that reassurance, he relaxed and rejoined the negotiations.

I tell my wife, "If you ever want to see me be the most petty, defensive person I can be, just give me the sense that you think I am a bad person at the core or that you are trying to change who I am." If she wants me to change something I *do* or *say*, I'm willing to give it a try. But not my core self.

Some years ago, several family therapists were watching a news program that showed protestors on both sides of the abortion debate screaming at each other across barriers. They suddenly realized that the opposing sides were a lot like the families they were seeing in family therapy. These families came into therapy polarized, usually doing a lot of yelling and very little listening. Family therapy is, in part, the art of getting people who are angry and alienated to sit down in the same room and begin to relate respectfully to one another. Usually, once that happens, we therapists can help these families solve the problems that brought them in.

These therapists decided to organize a project to bring together the "two sides" of the abortion debate in a respectful dialogue. What emerged was quite interesting. Once the opponents started listening to one another, they discovered more common ground than they thought they had. (For example, they all wanted to keep unwanted children from being brought into the world.) They also discovered, when they were given the opportunity to explore and converse in a nondefensive atmosphere, that many of them had more complex views than the either-or positions that they first espoused. (For example, some of the "antiabortion, pro-life" folks reluctantly admitted that there were circumstances in which they would support the right to abortion and some of the "abortion rights, pro-choice" folks admitted that there were some circumstances in which an abortion should be denied.) Once they included both the possibility that the "other side" wasn't necessarily all bad or evil and the possibility that there weren't just two sides to the issue, they could begin to work on possible solutions (better prenatal care and adoption and foster care services in their area). This is an example in which acknowledgment and inclusion helped bring about some change in a social context. This book, of course, is more about the personal context than the social, but individuals who learn to accept themselves and intimate others set the stage for similar breakthroughs among groups, countries, and cultures.

Summary of Method 2
ACKNOWLEDGE OTHERS' FEELINGS AND POINTS OF VIEW

Instead of agreeing or judging others' feelings or points of view as wrong or bad, just let them know that your hear and accept their inner experience.

Acknowledgment, Method 3:
Acknowledge the Facts and the Influence of the Past, Without Letting Them Determine the Present or Future

Even though solution-oriented therapy is focused on the present and the future, we acknowledge the importance of the past in people's lives. Where you have come from plays an important part in shaping who you are today. But the crucial point to make here is that the past, although it influences you, does not need to determine what you do from now on.

I heard a story from Steve Wolin, an acquaintance of mine. Steve is a psychiatrist who specializes in working with families and children affected by alcoholism. One day a young man came to Steve for help. The young man, sixteen years old, had been brought in by the parents of his girlfriend, who were paying for the treatment. He had had a very dysfunctional upbringing. His parents were using drugs and alcohol and were neglecting their four children. The kids had little to eat and weren't clothed or sheltered adequately. As you might imagine, their lives had been pretty chaotic up to that point. The young man was living at his girlfriend's house, as her parents, once they learned of his home situation, had taken him under their wing.

When Steve told the boy he was very lucky to have found a

girlfriend with such nice parents, the boy casually replied that it was no accident, as he had had to go through several other girlfriends until he had found one whose parents had liked him and were willing to help. He had also taken a job after school to earn money to help his younger siblings still at home. Steve was amazed that the young man had such resilience and began to study other children who had thrived despite coming from such difficult backgrounds. He found many other examples of such children.

The point I am making here is that your history does not determine your future. This does not mean that we aren't influenced by our past. Of course we are. But we aren't predestined or determined purely by our genetics or our background to go in any particular direction. It is important, again, to acknowledge the hurts and hardships of your past without letting them control your future.

Summary of Method 3

ACKNOWLEDGE THE FACTS AND THE INFLUENCE OF THE PAST, WITHOUT LETTING THEM DETERMINE THE PRESENT OR FUTURE

The past certainly has an influence on us, but we don't have to let the past write the story of our future or have it make us act any certain way in the present. By acknowledging what has happened in the past, we can face the past without having it dominate our present or future.

FOUR STEPS OF ACKNOWLEDGMENT

Now that you have seen some specific examples of how acknowledgment can be a catalyst for change, let's take a step-by-step approach to the process of acknowledgment. There are four steps or levels to acknowledgment, whether on a personal or social level: (1) acknowledging, (2) including, (3) valuing, and (4) embracing.

Step 1: Acknowledging

The first is just noting that something is there to be acknowledged: a feeling, a thought, another person, or a social inequity. This may mean noting it to yourself or to others, depending on the situation. This step I call *acknowledging.*

I remember hearing a story from a man who was using acknowledgment to help him change his temper, which had often gotten him in trouble. One day, he was driving along the highway, late for a business appointment, and he felt his car tire going flat. He stopped, got out, looked at the tire, and began to get angry. He thought, *Why did this have to happen now? I'm already late.* But, remembering to merely acknowledge, he stopped himself and thought, *I'm late and I have a flat tire.* Next he opened the trunk to get out his jack and spare tire. Just then it started to rain. He thought, *I'm late, I have a flat tire, and it is raining.* And he began laughing. He realized that getting angry wouldn't actually change the tire or make him any less late. So he might as well just acknowledge the truth of the matter and change the tire.

He could just as easily accepted himself for getting angry or being frustrated. Any acknowledgment may be a step out of the problem.

Step 2: Including

The next step is making room for or including whatever is there. The Ku Klux Klan takes note of the fact that there are blacks or Catholics in our society, but it doesn't have room for them; it does not want them included. Fundamentalist Christians think that people of different faiths or with no religious faith are wrong and bad. ACLU folks think that people who want to ban flag burnings or have prayer in school are an evil empire. "Those people" are seen as different and bad, and they don't belong.

On a more personal note, you may know that you get angry sometimes, but you don't want anger to be part of your life. You have no room for anger. If you don't include it, however, either you will be missing a crucial part of your experience that sometimes helps you or you will occasionally become enraged out of all proportion to the situation because you don't have much experience with handling your anger.

The step to take to counter this exclusion is *including.* Include feelings; include other people who are different from you; include contradictions within you and other things in your life that perhaps you haven't been making room for. Remember that including does not necessarily mean agreeing, but it does entail accepting the reality and validity of the feeling, the thought, the other person, or the situation.

Step 3: Valuing

The next step is moving up from making room for to actually valuing something or someone. Affirmative action plans in business acknowledge social inequities in hiring and promotion, and they make room for minorities and women in the workplace; but diversity programs actually value the contributions of different races and genders. When you can begin to value your emotions, including anger, sadness, and other so-called negative emotions, you have moved to this level. You can find the good in them, in the contributions that they make to your life.

Step 4: Embracing

The next step is embracing or incorporating something or someone into your life. The writer Herman Hesse said, "Love your suffering. Do not resist it; do not flee from it. It is only your aversion that hurts—nothing else." Embracing involves welcoming whatever feeling or experience or point of view enters your life. This goes a bit beyond just acknowledging, including, and valuing. You are actually joyfully going toward those aspects of your life that you have been dreading or avoiding. Bring on the failure, because without it I will never learn anything new or succeed. Bring on the tears; they let me know I am alive.

ACKNOWLEDGMENT AND ACCOUNTABILITY

One more point about acknowledgment. What you experience does not need to determine what you do in your life. Some people have the idea that if they have a feeling or a fantasy, it determines who they are or demands that they act on it. If I let my feelings run the show, I never would have completed this book. If I let any one part of my experience dominate, I am not including my other parts. It would be as if I were trying to sail my ship across the ocean and my different parts were crew members. Suppose one crew member suddenly takes the wheel because he feels like going back home. Another has a friend on a nearby island, so he knocks the first fellow off the wheel and grabs it himself. The course of such a ship would look like the lives of some people I know, veering this way and that, never reaching their goals and desired destinations. Experience is a good compass but a poor captain. Feelings make good advisers but poor

THE FOUR STEPS OF ACKNOWLEDGMENT

Step 1: **Acknowledging**
Taking note of some feeling, perception, or person to yourself or others

Step 2 **Including**
Making room for some feeling, perception, or person

Step 3 **Valuing**
Acknowledging the value in some feeling, perception, or person

Step 4 **Embracing**
Welcoming some feeling, perception, or person

masters. Acknowledge your experience and feelings, but don't let them determine what you do or stop you from where you have decided to go.

My friend Jerry wanted to run a marathon. He had been a runner for quite some time, but he had never run a marathon. He knew enough about running to know that he could seriously injure himself if he didn't train and prepare properly by running enough extra miles to gradually build his body up for this grueling endurance test. But he found that time and time again, he would fall off his training schedule. Finally he asked for my help.

I asked him to describe how he fell off his training schedule. He said that as the training schedule grew more lengthy and taxing, he would argue with himself in the morning when it was time to get up and start his run. The alarm clock would ring, and he would feel tired. A voice in his head would say, "You could sleep another thirty minutes and still get a good run in today." Or the voice would say,

"This is ridiculous. You're only running this marathon as a big ego trip." Or, "You won't be worth anything at work today if you don't get enough sleep." Or, "It's pretty cold out there this morning. Maybe you should skip today and do extra miles tomorrow." Sometimes Jerry would win the argument and get up and run, but often he would lose the argument and stay in bed. Interestingly, he told me that he always got up on time to do a regular run. I asked him how, and he replied that he never questioned it. He just got up and ran.

That helped me give him a plan. Jerry was to decide at the beginning of the month that he would train all month for the marathon. Then, unless he had an injury that would cause him harm if he ran with it, he would not get to "vote" on running in the morning. His only vote on whether or not to run would be in the evening at the first of the next month. Then he could rationally decide whether his goal to run a marathon—and the effort involved in it—was still worthwhile. Meanwhile, in the morning, when the alarm rang, he was not to engage in a discussion or struggle with his feelings or the voice inside his head.

As we sat at the finish line after his marathon, Jerry told me what had worked. The morning after we had made our plan, when the alarm rang, he heard the usual compelling arguments from the voice inside his head about why he should continue to sleep. And he felt like going back to sleep. As he listened to the voice, he swung his legs over the side of the bed and put on his running outfit. As he reached the door of his house, the voice was beginning to bargain: "Okay, if you go back and get fifteen more minutes of sleep, you can get up fifteen minutes earlier tomorrow and I won't complain." Jerry just opened the door, went outside, and began his stretches. As he ran, the voice gradually faded away. Every morning he went through the same routine. His previous mistake had been in letting the voice and his feelings run the show. Now he just acknowledged them and did what was right for him.

ACKNOWLEDGMENT EXERCISES

I've included some exercises you can do to develop Solution Key 3: Acknowledgment. Since this is a book about solutions and doing something different, it is important that you start to act on some of the possibilities suggested here. You may do so without using the exercises, however, finding your own way of incorporating these ideas into your life. So I want you to know up front that you are absolved of all guilt if you don't do the exercises.

Acknowledgment Exercise 1: Discovering Your Vulnerable Feelings and Giving Them a Voice

Examine your experience to find anything you have not been acknowledging to yourself about that experience, about your body, or about your core self. If you come across anything, ask yourself if you need to acknowledge it just to yourself or to someone else in order to make room for it and to value and embrace it.

If you can't think of anything, I can suggest a few corners you might look in. If you are a man, look in the direction of fear or other "vulnerable" feelings, such as sadness or weakness. We males get messages that it is not okay to be afraid, sad, or weak, so those feelings often remain unacknowledged for us. If you are a woman, look in the area of your body. How many of you would be willing to announce your dress size or weight to a group of acquaintances? I'm not saying that you should, but just examine whether you are feeling shame or denial about your body. If so, just acknowledge it, at least to yourself and maybe to someone else.

Next, do something that shows that you have room for or are including where you are or how you are. For example, if you are usually reticient to let yourself feel afraid, spend some time focusing on something of which you are afraid and just let yourself feel the feeling of fear.

One man did this by telling his partner that when they had a fight he was afraid she would leave him. She was surprised because during a fight all she heard from him was anger. She never glimpsed his fear or suspected that he was afraid. After that, she saw him in a new light during an argument, and once she reached out her hand to reassure him while they were having a heated discussion. He immediately softened, and they were able to settle the issue they had disagreed about.

A woman told me that after doing this exercise, she immediately went out and bought three new professional-looking outfits to wear to work. She had been wearing the same two ill-fitting, worn outfits for some time, waiting until she lost weight and got back to her "real weight" before she bought new clothes. As soon as she bought clothes in the size she was at the moment, she felt better about herself and lost a little weight. Never underestimate the power of acknowledgment.

Acknowledgment Exercise 2: Breaking Free from Compulsions and Addictions by Separating Your Feelings from Your Actions

To introduce this exercise, I need to tell you a little story. I once read an editorial that was written by a reader of one of the weekly newsmagazines and published in a "My Turn" feature. It was entitled something like "Come On, Fatties." Not a very nice title. But I was intrigued by how the writer was going to justify such a rude title, so I read on. The man recounted how he had been overweight since childhood and had been on every diet program that he could find. The diets had worked to varying degrees and for varying lengths of time, but ultimately he had regained the weight he lost and sometimes gained even more. He would get over-

Solution Key 3

ACKNOWLEDGE YOUR FEELINGS AND THE PAST, WITHOUT LETTING THEM DETERMINE YOUR ACTIONS IN THE PRESENT OR THE FUTURE

Method 1: Acknowledge your own experience, feelings, and self.

Method 2: Acknowledge others' feelings and points of view.

Method 3: Acknowledge the facts and the influence of the past without letting them determine the present or future.

whelming feelings of anxiety when he did not eat, although sometimes it was clear he was not really hungry when he ate. After getting discouraged with other people's solutions to weight problems, he decided he would try his own approach. The next time he felt anxious, he would just sit through it and not do anything. The first time he did it, he sat through four or five hours of emotional terror. He had no idea what he was afraid of or anxious about. It was just vague, free-floating anxiety and terror. But he resisted eating or doing anything else to escape what he was experiencing. Finally the anxiety and terror subsided, and he found he did not want to overeat. After that, every chance he could, he just sat and experienced his anxiety rather than eating to avoid it. His compulsive eating diminished to the point where he lost weight and kept it off. He had become convinced that all overweight people were rationalizing away the problem by saying, "I have a slow metabolism," or "It's all in your genes or your set point; you can't really change your weight all that much." While I think he made an unwarranted jump from his own experience to the entire group of people who weigh more than they think they should, his story gives a good basis for this exercise.

Focus on one area of your life in which things are not working for you because you are doing something compulsively or addictively. Your compulsion or addiction could be food or drugs or alcohol or chewing your nails or picking your face—anything that you feel compelled to do and that isn't good for you. Then, when you feel compelled to engage in the troublesome behavior, just let yourself notice and experience whatever emotions, thoughts, fantasies, or impulses you have concerning it, without having to do anything about them.

Beyond Positive Thinking

BALANCING ACKNOWLEDGMENT AND POSSIBILITY

Sometimes when I teach workshops on the solution-oriented approach, people come up during breaks and tell me that they really like the approach because it is so positive. I shudder a bit when I hear this. I understand what they mean. Traditional approaches to therapy can be negative and discouraging. But I am concerned that people will think all one has to do to make a better life is to "think positively." This can lead to minimizing the real problems that we face. To me, positive thinking is like seeing a pile of manure, covering it with a gold covering and calling it gold. It may look good for a time, but if you poke the pile, you find that it is still manure underneath the nice-looking exterior. Of course, negative thinking is just as bad: you think that everything is manure and there is nothing anyone can do about it. In this approach, we maintain that it is important both to acknowledge the problem (the manure) and to do what you can to change the situation (turn it into compost, clean it up, or whatever else might help). This is different from positive thinking, in that it acknowledges problems and barriers to change at the same time as it acknowledges possibilities for change. If you don't do *both*, you risk getting stuck in negative, bitter thinking or getting caught unawares when unrealistic, pie-in-the-sky plans go wrong.

CHAPTER 5

WHAT YOU FOCUS ON EXPANDS

Shifting Attention

The greatest gift you can give another is the purity of your attention.

—Richard Moss, M.D.

A powerful way to change the viewing of the problem is simply to shift what you are paying attention to in the situation.

My teacher, the psychiatrist Milton Erickson, discovered by doing hypnosis that changing attention was a powerful way to solve problems. He would have a person in an hypnotic trance who was suffering from chronic pain—say, from arthritis—shift his or her attention to the parts of the body that didn't hurt. Perhaps the left big toe didn't hurt at the moment when all the other joints ached. With hypnotic suggestion, Erickson could keep people's attention focused on the more comfortable parts of their experience. In this chapter, we will use the same principle of shifting attention to some other aspect of your situation or your experience, but without the need to use hypnosis.

One day Erickson's young son, Robert, fell on the sidewalk outside their home. He cut his mouth and was bleeding heavily when his parents arrived on the scene, alerted by his cries of pain and fear. Erickson immediately said, "Robert, it hurts. It hurts real bad. Real bad. I wonder when it's going to stop hurting. Right now it hurts; it just hurts. When is it going to stop hurting?" This caught Robert's attention. At first, he was only attending to the pain, but now he also began wondering when the pain would stop. He stopped crying as he wondered about that. By that time, his parents had gotten him to the bathroom, where they were washing his mouth so Erickson could determine whether or not stitches would be required. As the blood ran from Robert's mouth into the sink, Erickson said to his wife, "Look at that blood, Mother. That's good red healthy blood! That'll clean that wound out really well. Look at the color of that blood." Of course, Robert was also looking at the blood. Instead of being captured by his pain and fear, he was fascinated attending to his "good red healthy blood." After the wound was washed out, it became clear that Robert would need stitches. So Erickson began to tell Robert that he needed stitches and reminded him that his brother had gotten stitches last year when he had been hurt. "I wonder whether you are going to win the stitches contest, Robert, and get more than your brother got. He had six stitches. All you would need is seven to win the contest." When they arrived at the emergency room, the attending physician was amazed at how quietly this young boy sat while he was being cleaned and stitched up. All Robert said through his stitched-up mouth at the end of the procedure was "How many stitches did I get?" "Nine," he was told. And he gave a lopsided smile through the wound. That is the power of changing your attention.

Solution Key 4
SHIFT YOUR ATTENTION

What you focus your attention on tends to increase and expand in both your awareness and your life.

When you are having problems, it is usually because you are attending to the same thing over and over again. To solve the problem, change what you are attending to in the situation. To do this, ask yourself: What am I consistently paying attention to in this the problem? What am I focused on that is not helpful? Find anything else to attend to and begin to focus on that.

Really, this whole book is an invitation for you to shift your attention from analysis, explanations, and problems to actions that can help solve problems. Our culture is steeped in problem-orientation. We have an idea that when problems happen, they are caused or determined by the past and that things are just the way they are, set in concrete. If you simply do or think something different, however, many things can change. If you change your focus from problems to solutions, things can change even more quickly.

How do you use this solution key to solve your problem? There are several methods.

Shifting Attention, Method 1: Change Your Sensory Channel

Usually one of the easiest shifts is to attend to something different in your sensory experience (what you see, hear, smell, taste, touch). Shift from seeing things to listening, or from listening to touching. During an argument, close your eyes and really listen to your partner.

I had a client who was bingeing and vomiting. Together we

discovered that one of the triggers for her compulsive eating was attending some social gathering where food was available. She would notice the food right away and become drawn to it. She would vow to herself that she would not eat any of the fatty items, but would find herself eating compulsively throughout the party. On the way home, feeling guilty and out of control, she would buy more food and binge on it. When she arrived home, stuffed and feeling horrible, she would make herself vomit, afraid that she would gain too much weight from her overeating.

She happened to be a very gregarious, social person, so I suggested that the next time she attended a party, she should focus on the faces of three people who were there. She was to pick out the three friendliest-looking people and introduce herself to them. After that, she could eat all she wanted. Of course, she never got to the food table at subsequent events, as she invariably met some interesting people as the result of her sensory shift and became immersed in conversations that shifted her attention from food to people.

Summary of Method 1:
CHANGE YOUR SENSORY CHANNEL

Shift your attention from one of your ways of gathering information from the world (such as seeing, hearing, touching, tasting, or smelling) to a different input channel.

Shifting Attention, Method 2: Expand Your Focus of Attention

If you have a problem in which you are plagued by a recurring memory, rather than trying to get rid of the memory, try expanding it. Remember what happened before and after the incident you are focused on. Look around the place in which the incident occurred and notice anything that was not really in the foreground for you before.

I counseled a man who had a fear of flying. He had developed this phobia after taking a particularly scary and difficult flight during a winter snowstorm. The plane ran into some turbulence, which tossed it around in the snowy skies. My client had become convinced that the plane would crash. Ever since that flight, he had been terrified to go up in a plane. He occasionally had to travel for his job. If he had a trip planned, he would develop diarrhea for weeks before the flight and suffer panic attacks both before and during the trip.

As we worked on resolving this fear, he told me about the scene that would play over and over again in his mind whenever he thought about flying. He would remember being on the plane during the snowstorm. The woman next to him had noticed his panic and had tried to calm him down. But after some minutes of talking, he had begun to convince the woman that the plane was going to crash and she became frightened as well. Her husband, sitting on her other side, had to calm her fears. So now in addition to feeling terrified, he had felt guilty about scaring this nice woman who had been trying to help him. He could vividly recall his feelings of panic and guilt, his hands gripping the armrests of his seat, and his thought, "I'll never make it out of this plane alive!" Every time he thought about flying he went right back to this terrifying scene.

As we talked in greater detail about this first fearful incident of flying, he was surprised to find that he began to remember other things about the incident. He recalled one man across the aisle from him who was calmly reading and another several aisles away who slept through the entire terrifying ride. As we continued to talk about it, he recounted how the plane had finally landed and he had gotten up and walked off the plane, grateful to be alive. A look of wonder came across his face as he remembered this part of the trip. "I did make it off that plane alive!" he exclaimed. After that, whenever he started to panic about an airplane trip, he would deliberately change his attention from focusing on the scariest part of that memory to the part in which he was walking off the plane. This reduced his fear enough so he was able to fly with relative ease, especially after several more comfortable flights.

A woman who was trying to lose weight was told to go to the supermarket and see how many new foods she could notice. She reported that she was surprised by how many items there were that she had never noticed. She typically bought the same items on each trip to the store. After discovering the variety of new foods available, she decided that instead of overeating, she would begin to try new foods as a way of satisfying her interest in food. That way, she was able to enjoy food while losing weight rather than having to restrict her food intake.

Summary of Method 2

EXPAND YOUR FOCUS OF ATTENTION

Instead of the usual narrowly focused attention, broaden your view and search for aspects of the situation you never really noticed before.

Shifting Attention, Method 3: Shift Your Focus from the Past to the Present

Another client was having intrusive memories, while she was having sex with her husband, of being sexually abused by her father. These flashbacks from childhood had come to dominate the couple's sex life, so that sex had become an unhappy experience for them both. But the solution turned out to be surprisingly simple. The couple, it seemed, always had sex with the lights out. I suggested that whenever the wife started to have memories of sexual abuse, they turn on the lights. She was then to look at her husband and to touch his face. He was to say something to her. All this helped shift her attention from the past and her horrible memories, to the present and to her husband, who had never been abusive to her. After she changed her attention, they could continue, with the lights either on or off, stopping to reorient her attention only if the flashbacks occurred again. After they practiced this procedure several times, the memories became less intrusive and their sex life improved.

Summary of Method 3

SHIFT YOUR FOCUS FROM THE PAST TO THE PRESENT

Instead of focusing on what happened, focus on what is happening right now.

Shifting Attention, Method 4:
Shift Your Focus from the Present or the Past to the Future

Chapter 6 is entirely devoted to this method, so here I'll just give you a quick example.

A client of mine was obsessing about her last boyfriend. Even though she had broken off the relationship because of her partner's physical abuse and his risky drug-taking, she still felt that it was the best relationship she had ever had or would have. It was much like other abusive and dangerous relationships that she had had with other men in her life. We began to discuss what kind of relationship she would have if she broke her usual pattern of relationships with dangerous men. As we discussed it more and more, she began to get interested in finding a relationship like the one in her future-oriented image. We talked about the steps she would take. The first step, she agreed, was to begin to notice men she had never given a second thought to in the past, because they weren't her "type." She decided that she would begin to date men to whom she was not initially attracted and find out as she got to know them whether they offered more of what she hoped for in a relationship.

Summary of Method 4

SHIFT YOUR FOCUS FROM THE PRESENT OR THE PAST TO THE FUTURE

Focus on what you would like to have happen instead of what has happened or is happening.

Shifting Attention, Method 5: Shift from Your Internal Experience to the External Environment or to Other People

In a situation that is making you fearful, rather than focusing on your fear, try just touching the items around you and paying attention to their textures. If you are frequently anxious, try doing an hour or two of volunteer work at a local shelter for the homeless.

Milton Erickson, my teacher, once suggested to a young man, David, who was spending his time depressed at home all alone, that he try going to the public library and being depressed there. David agreed to try it. Instead of just sitting there dwelling on how depressing life was, David decided he would look up some material on exploring caves, something he had always had an interest in but had never pursued. While he was in the section on cave exploration, another young man approached David and asked if he was interested in spelunking. David said he was, and that led to a conversation that eventually led to the two men going cave exploring together. As David made this new friend and began getting out more, he became less depressed.

Summary of Method 5

SHIFT FROM YOUR INTERNAL EXPERIENCE TO THE EXTERNAL ENVIRONMENT OR TO OTHER PEOPLE

Get out of your insides and focus out on the world.

Shifting Attention, Method 6: Shift from Focusing on Others or the External Environment to Focusing on Your Inner World

A client of mine was so busy with a demanding work life and family activities that he began to feel as if he wasn't really living, just doing duties and existing. He arranged a weekend retreat for silent meditation. During this time, he discovered some serious problems in his marriage that he had been avoiding or denying. As he engaged in dealing with these problems, he found himself starting to feel alive again. He began working less and exercising more.

Summary of Method 6

SHIFT FROM FOCUSING ON OTHERS OR THE EXTERNAL ENVIRONMENT TO FOCUSING ON YOUR INNER WORLD

Move your awareness to what is going on in your feelings or inner life rather than focusing on what others are saying or doing or on what is happening in the world around you.

Shifting Attention, Method 7: Focus on What Has Worked (or Is Working) Rather Than on What Hasn't (or Isn't)

This is ultimately what the whole book is about and what Chapter 2 detailed, but there are small ways to use this method that can generate positive results. For example, if you are focused on the frowns on people's faces when you are giving a speech, try finding one person in the group who is smiling or nodding as you are talking and focus on him or her. Or you can focus on catching your child, your spouse, or your employee doing something right rather than commenting on what he or she has done wrong.

I heard a story of a minister who was always under pressure to do more in his congregation, even though he worked many more than forty hours a week at his job. He was also regularly criticized by some members of the congregation for one thing or another. (He was too liberal or too conservative, or he should be organizing more youth events.) He began what he called his "grace file." This was a folder in which he kept the nice notes that people had given him through the years, thanking him for some kind words, for a particularly moving sermon, or for counseling that had saved a marriage. When he felt hassled, discouraged, or unappreciated, he would go to his study and read from his grace file, returning to his work with renewed vigor.

Summary of Method 7

FOCUS ON WHAT HAS WORKED (OR IS WORKING) RATHER THAN WHAT HASN'T (OR ISN'T)

Notice solutions and positive events and actions more than problems and negative events and activities.

Shifting Attention, Method 8: Shift from Thinking or Feeling to Action

If you are stuck on some thought or feeling, focus on an action you could take that would be either beneficial to resolving the troubling feeling or thought, or beneficial in general in your life.

A man consulted me who was unhappy with his job. He had been unhappy with it for some time but had never really done anything to change it. He wanted to work for himself, but as soon as he started to think about that prospect, either he would get dreamy and spend his time fantasizing about what a great life he would have when he finally worked for himself, or he would get anxious and decide that it was too risky a move and that he would never succeed.

We made an agreement that every time he grew unhappy with his job, instead of fantasizing or getting anxious, he would begin to make specific plans for action and take specific steps (like calling people he knew who might give him consulting contracts) that could both lead in the direction of his dreams and decrease his anxiety about failing.

Summary of Method 8:
CHANGE YOUR FOCUS FROM THINKING OR FEELING TO ACTION

Instead of focusing on your inner life, move into action.

Shifting Attention, Method 9: Ask Solution-Oriented Questions

If they can get you asking the wrong questions, they don't have to worry about the answers.

—Thomas Pynchon

Instead of focusing on asking yourself "problem" questions—questions like "Why am I having this problem?" "What's wrong with me?" "What did I do to deserve this?" or "What in my childhood or my genetics or my biology caused me to be this way?"—I suggest that you focus on asking variations of the same question: "What do I keep doing and thinking and attending to that is not helpful, and what else could I do or think or focus on to change the situation?"

As a general rule, questions that ask *why* can lead you in the wrong direction, seeking explanations and going over the same territory again and again. Of course, they don't always do this. Sometimes a *why* question can lead you in a useful direction or help you sort out a situation you are in. But I would recommend asking more questions that begin with words like *how* or *what* instead. For example, instead of asking yourself *Why do these terrible things always happen to me?* or *Why do I always get dumped on in relationships?* ask yourself more productive questions such as, *What can I do to ɪis situation?* or *How can I make it less likely that I will get ɪn in future relationships?*

If you are prone to ask yourself problem questions, try any of these as an alternative:

1. What can I see and hear about this situation (i.e., what are the facts), and what conclusions (stories, judgments, criticisms) have I made from those facts?
2. If I'm going to have to go through this anyway, what can I get out of it?
3. What do I have to do to make things more the way I want them to be?
4. What am I willing to stop doing in order to have things be more the way I want them to be?
5. Is this where I want to put my energy or attention? If not, where would I rather focus my energy or attention?
6. Is there anything I can do about this right now? If so, what is the first step I will take? If not, how can I come to accept and make peace with what I can't change right now?
7. Where are my moments or places of choice in this situation?
8. What's the best way I've ever handled a situation like this before?

When the computer crashed in the business he owned, Chris's first tendency was to start yelling and throwing things. That was his typical reaction to crises, and this was a bad crisis. Chris hadn't backed up the data on the computer for over eight months. The business was booming, and he hadn't had time to keep up with administrative duties. Customers were calling, asking where their orders were. In addition, it was a Friday and Chris had given his vice president the day off, since she would have to run things while Chris attended a family wedding that weekend in which he was to be the best man. To top things off, two key employees had quit unexpectedly earlier that week, and he hadn't yet found replacements.

Chris's first thought was, *Why does this always happen to me?* Then he shifted to a solution question: *Is there anything I can do about this right now?* He telephoned his vice president, and she agreed to come in and help get things straightened out. He contacted a computer consultant who promised he would get the computers up and running that day if it was at all possible. By the time his vice president arrived, Chris was feeling a bit less panicky. They sat down to talk and his vice president, who tended to be a calm and collected person, said, "Chris, what do we need to do to turn this crisis into an opportunity to have fun?"

Chris was a bit stunned. He was a fun-loving guy who had done his best after he started his company to make it a fun place for himself and his employees to work, but he had never considered having fun during a crisis. Still, he was willing to consider the idea. They started brainstorming ways to make this crisis fun. Chris decided to wear a dunce cap all day so the employees could see what a dummy he was for not backing up the computer data. He wrote fifty times on the company blackboard, "I will back up every day and keep copies at home and in a safe-deposit box." Strangely, just as they were getting into the fun of things, a job applicant showed up and they hired him on the spot, since he was perfect for the job. The consultant arrived, got the computers up and running, and was able to save all the data. As soon as Chris started asking himself more solution-oriented questions, things turned around. And even if they hadn't, he'd have had some fun out of it all. He who laughs last. . . .

Solution Key 4

SHIFT YOUR ATTENTION

Method 1: **Change your sensory channel.**

Switch between your visual, auditory, tactile, olfactory, and gustatory senses. Notice which one you are using the most in the problem situation and change to another one. Or focus on something else within the same sensory channel.

Method 2: **Expand your focus of attention.**

Pay attention to things you haven't really noticed in the problem situation.

Method 3: **Shift from focusing on the past to focusing on the present.**

Focus on what is happening right where you are now rather than evoking or remembering the past.

Method 4: **Shift from focusing on the present or the past to focusing on the future.**

Shift from what you remember or what is happening now to what you would like to be doing or feeling in the future.

Method 5: **Shift from focusing on your internal experience to focusing on the external environment or other people.**

Instead of focusing on what is going on inside you (your thoughts, feelings, fantasies, experiences), focus instead on someone else or what is going on around you.

Method 6: **Shift from focusing on others or the external environment to focusing on your inner world.**

If tuning in to the external world or to others is what you usually do in a problem situation, try withdrawing your attention from the external and tuning in to your inner world.

Method 7: **Focus on what has worked (or is working) rather than what hasn't (or isn't).**
Focus on what is working or has worked for you in this situation or similar situations in the past.

Method 8: **Change your focus from thinking or feeling to action.**
Instead of focusing on your inner life, move out into the world of action.

Method 9: **Ask solution-oriented questions.**
Examine the typical questions you are asking yourself or others about the situation. Start asking more useful questions; that is, ask questions that help you feel better about the situation or change it for the better. In general, *what* and *how* questions tend to be more productive than *why* questions.

Summary of Method 9

ASK SOLUTION-ORIENTED QUESTIONS

Change the kinds of questions you are asking or living with from ones that do not lead anywhere or that make you feel worse to ones that open up new possibilities or lead to solutions or good feelings.

Shifting Attention Exercise

CHANGE PROBLEM QUESTIONS TO SOLUTION QUESTIONS

Consider a typical problematic situation. Write down the typical questions you are asking yourself or others about it. Examine these questions closely. Does asking them help you feel better or worse? Does asking them help move you forward to where you want to be or merely give you a good explanation for why you are stuck or can't change? If your questions are not helping you, try some of the alternative questions listed above or come up with some more helpful questions yourself.

CHAPTER 6

IF YOU DON'T HAVE A DREAM, HOW YOU GONNA MAKE A DREAM COME TRUE?

Using the Future to Solve Problems

> My interest is in the future because I am going to spend the rest of my life there.
>
> —Charles F. Kettering

In 1990, the psychiatrist Viktor Frankl delivered the keynote address at a conference held in Anaheim, California. As 7,000 people listened, Frankl told the compelling story of his life. He described the terrible things that happened to him while he was imprisoned in a Nazi death camp, and how he had nearly died many times. He was physically and psychologically abused and tortured. During his talk, Frankl described one day in particular that seemed to be etched deeply within him.

On a wintry day in Poland he was being marched through a field with a group of other prisoners. He was dressed in thin clothing, with no socks, and he had holes in his shoes. Very ill from malnutrition and mistreatment, he began to cough. The cough was so severe that he fell to his knees. A guard came over and told him to get up and keep walking, but his cough was so intense and debilitating that he could not even answer. The guard began to beat him with a club and told him that he would be left to die if he did not get up. Frankl—who had witnessed this being done to other prisoners—knew the guard was deadly serious. Sick, in pain, and being hit, he thought, "This is it for me." He didn't have the wherewithal to get up.

There he was on the ground, in no condition to go on, and all of the sudden he was no longer in Poland. Instead, he found himself imagining himself standing at a lectern in postwar Vienna giving a lecture on "The Psychology of Death Camps." He had an audience of two hundred rapt with attention. The lecture was one that he had been working out the whole time he had been in the death camp. He spoke about how some people seem to survive the experience better than others, psychologically and emotionally. It was a brilliant lecture, all taking place in his mind's eye and ear. He was no longer half-dead in the field but living in the lecture. During the lecture, Frankl told the imaginary audience about the day he was in that field being beaten and was certain he didn't have the strength to get up and keep walking.

Then, wonder of wonders, he told his imagined audience, he was able to stand up. The guard stopped beating him and he began, haltingly at first, then with more strength, to walk. As he was imagining describing this to his audience, his body got up and began to walk. He continued to imagine this lecture all the while he was doing the work detail and through the cold march back to the death camp. He collapsed into his bunk, imagining ending this brilliantly clear speech and receiving a standing ovation. Many years later and thousands of miles away—in 1990 in Anaheim, California—he received a standing ovation from 7,000 people after this speech.

What did Viktor Frankl do that most people with problems

don't do? He vividly imagined a future in which his problems were resolved and then worked backward to the present to determine what he would need to do in order to make that future a reality.

If you are stuck with a problem, just turning your gaze from the past to a future in which the problem is no longer with you is a major change in the viewing of the problem. Then, of course, you have to work backward to the present to figure out what you could do to make that future a reality, rather than just an appealing fantasy. It is important to acknowledge the past rather than to deny or ignore it. But it is just as crucial to focus your attention on where you'd like to be.

Solution Key 5

IMAGINE A FUTURE THAT LEADS BACK TO SOLUTIONS IN THE PRESENT

Recently, I read an article about the Internet in which the author said that the most important thing for business in the future, given all the new media, was going to be a fight to capture buyers' attention. Attention would be the most valuable currency of the future, he predicted. What you attend to influences and guides your actions. Just ask all those marketers who are trying to capture your eyes and ears with their commercials. So where are you putting your attention in regard to your problem? If you are not focused mostly on the future, you are not likely to solve the problem.

Using the Future, Method 1: Use "Possibility" Talk and "Positive Expectancy" Talk

How to Use "Possibility" Talk Instead of Problem Language

One way we stay stuck in our problems is by speaking about them in a problem-oriented and past-oriented way. When we use discouraging language, we are inadvertently channeling our thinking and feelings away from the possibility that the future can be better and that we can solve our problems. But language is also a powerful tool to change the viewing of a problem. Using "possibility" talk naturally creates a sense of choice and change:

- Talk about problems in the past tense rather than the present or future tense—"I have been depressed," rather than "I am depressed" or "I'll be depressed the rest of my life." This leaves the present and future open to new possibilities.
- Avoid absolute, all-or-nothing words and phrases. Words like "never," "always," "no one," "everyone," and "nothing," when used in a negative, discouraging way tend to channel your thinking into impossibility and block access to hope and creative thinking. Turn an absolute or generalized statement or question into a partial statement or question. Instead of saying, "We never get along," say, "We usually don't get along," or "Most of the time we argue."
- Avoid talking about yourself or others as being the problem. These labels can stick like crazy glue. Saying, "I'm a depressive person," or "She is a complainer," distorts things and can keep you and others from seeing that there are other qualities and aspects to

yourself or other people. You can say instead, "I suffer from depression," or "She tends to complain." Instead of saying, "I'm a procrastinator," you could try saying, "I have usually procrastinated."

How to Use "Positive Expectancy" Talk

Another way to move your attention more to the future and to solutions is to use what I call "*positive expectancy*" *talk*. Our language often reflects our expectations about the future. You can help seed the future you want by using "expectancy" talk to create the sense that a better future is possible and even likely for you.

If you are using language like, "Things will never get better," or "What's going to go wrong next," or "He'll never change," you are expecting the future to be the same as or worse than the present. And because your expectations influence the future, you are likely to inadvertently bring about more of the same or worse. If you believe things won't change, you are likely to keep doing what you have always done. If you believe things will get worse, you are likely to act in such a way as to unwittingly make them worse. You create a self-fulfilling prophecy.

Many years ago, an experiment was done in which some teachers were told that they had a difficult group of students that year. Other teachers were told that they had a gifted group of highly motivated kids. In truth, each teacher had a regular mix of students. But by the end of the year, the "troubled" students were getting worse grades, had more behavioral problems, and had lower test scores. The so-called gifted kids were doing better in all those areas. The only difference between the groups was the teachers' expectations.

I told this story while I was teaching in the public school system in Memphis some years ago, and in turn I was told a story (perhaps apocryphal) that was legendary in the school district. It seems that one year, there was a class of students who were so unruly that they burned out two different teachers. One teacher took early retirement and the other decided to get out of teaching altogether. This class was so bad that substitute teachers began to refuse to take it. So the district called a teacher who had applied for a job but hadn't made the cut that year. They asked her if she would be willing to come in and finish out the year in return for the promise of a full-time position the next year. She eagerly accepted. The principal decided not to warn the teacher about the class, afraid that she would be scared off if she heard what she was up against. After the new teacher had been on the job for a month, the principal sat in on a class to see how things were going. To his amazement, the students were well-behaved and enthusiastic. After the students had filed out of the classroom, the principal stayed behind to congratulate the teacher on a job well done. She thanked him but insisted that he deserved thanks for giving her such a special class, such a great class, for her first assignment. The principal hemmed and hawed and told her that he really didn't deserve any thanks. She laughed and told him, "You see, I discovered your little secret on my first day here. I looked in the desk drawer and found the list of the students' IQ scores. I knew I had a challenging group of kids here, so bright and rambunctious that I would really have to work to make school interesting for them because they are so intelligent." She slid the drawer open and the principal saw the list with the students' names and the numbers 136, 145, 127, 128, and so on written next to the names. He exclaimed, "Those aren't their IQ scores—those are their locker numbers!" Too late. The teacher had already expected the students to be bright and gifted—and they had responded positively to her positive view and her positive handling of them.

You can deliberately create a context for positive expectancy by using "positive expectancy" talk:

- Use "positive expectancy" talk to anticipate solutions and prime the pump for possibilities. "*So far* I haven't been able to get that job I wanted," or "We haven't been able to figure out how to get along *yet*." "*When* I solve this problem, I'll be able to get along with others much better," instead of "*If* I solve this problem . . ."

- Use key phrases and words: *so far; yet; up until now; when; will.*

Summary of Method 1

USE "POSSIBILITY" TALK AND "POSITIVE EXPECTANCY" TALK

Talk about problems in the past tense; avoid absolute words and phrases; avoid talking about anyone as being the problem. Use expectations to create a sense of a better future and to anticipate solutions.

Using the Future, Method 2: Living As If—Create or Evoke a Compelling Future

> If you are hopeful, of course, you can take action. The miracle occurs when you don't feel much hope, yet you push yourself into action anyway. Perhaps it is the brain, stimulated by the action, that brings you back to hope. I don't know why it works. I just know that it does.
>
> —Shari Lewis, quoted in Rabbi Maurice Lamm's *The Power of Hope*

Another method for creating a future filled with possibilities is to imagine a future in which the problem is resolved—as if you can see it in a crystal ball or as if a miracle has occurred—and then act as if that future will be yours. What will you be doing then?

What would you have to do right now in order to make that future happen?

A group of therapists in Milwaukee came up with an intriguing method of creating this solution-oriented view of the future. They began to ask people with problems to imagine that while they were sleeping that night, a miracle occurred in which their problems were removed from their lives. Of course, since the people were asleep when the miracle happened, they didn't know it had happened. Then—and this is the crucial part—they asked these people to tell them what would be the first thing they would do the next day when they awoke that would tell them that the miracle had occurred. They found that people, when asked this question, often had a very good idea of what actions and ways of thinking they would use when they were out from under the problem.

It is important to remember that method 2 does not involve hoping for a miracle to solve your problems—it means freeing your imagination and your actions from unnecessary limitations. There are three steps to using this method: (1) Get clear on what your future would look like without the problem or when you are living a satisfying and meaningful life. (2) Recognize and deal with the barriers to that better future. (3) Make an action plan to overcome any barriers and make that future become reality.

Step 1: Find a Vision for the Future

As you saw in Viktor Frankl's story, having a vision for the future can be invaluable in helping you solve your current problems and take steps to create a better future. The following questions may help you develop a clear vision of the future and your purpose in life. Answer any questions that help you gain a sense of purpose and possibilities for your future:

- What is your life's purpose?
- What kinds of things would you like to accomplish or have happen in your future?
- What dreams did you or do you have for your life?
- What are you here on the planet for?
- What are human beings on the planet for, in your view?
- What area do you think you could make a contribution in?
- What kinds of things compel you?
- What makes your heart sing?
- What kinds of things will you be doing when you have resolved this problem?
- How will you be different with other people when you no longer have this problem?
- How will others recognize that you no longer have this problem if you haven't told them it is gone?

I was consulting with a family whose fifteen-year-old son had become involved with gangs and drugs. He had previously been a good student, getting A's and B's. But since he had been in the gang and doing drugs, his grades had dropped until he had failed all his classes in the last semester. The boy told me that he hated school. I asked him what class he hated most and what class he hated least. English was the worst, he said, and art was the best. What did he like about art? I asked. "Well," he replied, "I'm the graffiti guy for the gang and I'm good at drawing. I got A's in my drawing projects in art class, but I hated the other stuff—art history, doing mobiles and sculptures, and things like that. So I still failed." I asked him how he planned to earn a living if he flunked out of high school. He didn't really have a plan, he said. "Can you make a living doing art?" I asked. "Sure," he said, "you can paint murals." "How do you get into that?" I wanted to know. He told me that a man from the community who painted murals had come to his art class the last year and told the students that he had more work than he could handle and would be willing to take on apprentices and help them get started doing murals for pay. "How do you get to be his apprentice?" I asked. "You have to be in school and getting passing grades," he replied. "Any interest in pursuing that?" I asked. "Yeah," he said. His parents almost fell off their chairs as he went on to discuss what he would need to do to succeed in school: stay away from the gang and stay off drugs. They had been lecturing him about those same things, and he had fought them all the way. But once he discovered his own motivation, he was able to solve his problems.

Step 2: Deal with and Dissolve Barriers to the Preferred Future

Once you discover or clarify your vision of the future, you may need to deal with actual or perceived barriers to getting there. Sometimes people know what they would like to do with their lives or what future they would like to have happen, but they cannot get there because they perceive insurmountable barriers in their way. They have fears of success or fears of failure. They think they are inadequate to the task of making the dream happen, or they think certain things must happen before they can begin to pursue their dreams. Sometimes there are very real barriers to achieving one's goals or realizing one's dreams.

Years ago, when I was just beginning to get a vision of the kind of contribution I thought I was called to make in my chosen field, I sought out the advice of an older, more successful therapist. I told him that I felt called to a mission to make therapy more respectful of clients and a more effective endeavor. I thought that to accomplish my mission, I would have to write books and teach workshops to reach the widest audience. He told me that one problem was that I had only a master's degree in a field that was dominated by Ph.D.s and M.D.s. He said that I would never be able to get a book published without getting a higher degree. I left that conversation shaken, because I felt I was ready to start immediately and did not want to spend more years in school. I persisted, and within two years I had a contract to write my first book. The book you are holding in your hands is my seventeenth, and I still have "only a master's degree," so I suppose my colleague was mistaken. Sometimes we perceive barriers where there are none. There are enough real barriers that adding to them from your fears or imagination or other people's beliefs only adds to your difficulties.

The following questions might prove helpful in identifying and surmounting real or imagined barriers.

- What, in your view, stops you from realizing your visions or getting to your goals?
- What are you afraid of?
- What do you believe must happen before you can realize your visions and goals? Is this really true, or is it just an idea that you or someone else has?
- What are the actions you haven't taken to make your dreams and visions come true?
- What are the real barriers you'll need to deal with to realize your dreams and visions?
- What would your role models, mentors, or people you admire do if they were you in order to realize this dream or vision?
- What are you not doing, feeling, or thinking that they would in this situation?
- What are you doing, feeling, or thinking that they wouldn't?

Step 3: Make an Action Plan to Reach the Preferred Future

> The best way to predict the future is to create it.
>
> —Peter Drucker

Solution Key 5

IMAGINE A FUTURE THAT LEADS BACK TO SOLUTIONS IN THE PRESENT

Method 1: **Use "possibility" and "positive expectancy" talk.** Stop talking in negative, discouraging ways that presume that the future you desire is impossible. Start talking as if the future you want is both possible and likely.

Method 2: **Living as if: Create or evoke a compelling future.** Envision a future in which your problem is resolved or in which you are living your dreams and your purpose in life, and then act as if that future were possible and likely. Challenge any barriers, real or imagined, that would prevent you from attaining this future.

Having a clear vision of the future is helpful—but clarity alone doesn't guarantee that this future will be achieved. You also need a plan of action. Viktor Frankl could not just imagine better days. He had to get up and walk that day in the snowy field. Then, when he finally emerged from the death camp, he had to begin to write books and give lectures.

A woman who was undergoing chemotherapy for cancer was convinced that she would die. She was very sick from the chemotherapy and then had become depressed. She had not been able to eat properly or keep food down—and food had previously been one of the joys of her life. After we talked about acting as if she would get well, I asked her what action she would be taking now if she were convinced she would get well. She said that she would be getting her cookbooks out and planning all the wonderful meals she would have when the chemotherapy was over and she was on the mend.

She went home after our meeting and began to read her cookbooks and plan some great meals. She found as she did so that she became more hopeful and less depressed. For the first time in months, she said, she could actually imagine this ordeal being over and surviving the cancer.

The following questions can help you begin to formulate and put into practice actions that can help create your preferred future:

- What could you do in the near future that would be steps toward realizing your visions and dreams?
- What would you do as soon as you close this book?
- What would you do tonight?
- What feeling would you have in your body as you took those steps?
- What would you be thinking that would help you take those steps?
- What images or metaphors are helpful to you in taking these steps?
- What's the first thing you would think or do when you are on the right track?
- Have you already done something that lets you know you are heading in the right direction?

Summary of Method 2

LIVING AS IF: CREATE OR EVOKE A COMPELLING FUTURE

Step 1: Find a vision for the future

If you don't know where you're going, you'll probably end up somewhere else. It's important to have a dream and a vision of where you'd like to be, even if it only involves a future without the problem or problems you are currently facing.

Step 2: Deal with and dissolve barriers to the preferred future

Get clear on what internal (imaginary) and real barriers you are facing that could stop you from reaching a better future or even trying to achieve such a future. Challenge the barriers by changing your actions or changing your thoughts.

Step 3: Make an action plan to reach the preferred future

Even if you aren't sure you can achieve your goal, you can begin to take actions as if the future you envision will come true.

Obviously, envisioning a future you want and starting to take actions toward it won't always lead to results; but if you decide the future you hope for is unattainable and don't take actions toward achieving that future, it is almost guaranteed that the better future won't arrive.

CHAPTER 7

REWRITING LIFE STORIES

Changing Problem Beliefs into Solution-Oriented Ideas

In recent years, social scientists have come to appreciate what political, religious, and military figures have long known; that stories (narratives, myths, or fables) constitute a uniquely powerful currency in human relationships. . . . And I suggest, further, that it is stories . . . of identity—narratives that help individuals think about and feel who they are, where they come from, and where they are headed—that constitute the single most powerful weapon in the leader's . . . arsenal.

—Howard Gardner, *Leading Minds: An Anatomy of Leadership*

When I was young, I was painfully shy. This was a constant source of frustration for me. I couldn't make friends very easily, ask girls for dates, or speak up in groups when I had something to say. I was lonely much of the time. Finally, when I was reading a book one day, I came across the idea that perhaps I wasn't shy—it was just that I had learned to "do shy." This idea appealed to me because it meant that there was hope that I could change things. If I had learned shy behaviors, I could learn "not shy" behaviors. I began to act in ways that were inconsistent with the old story I and others believed about me: that I was a shy person. I had heard all my life that I was shy. My family always described me that way. I had come to think of myself as shy. But now I realized that this might simply be a story: a made-up idea. Eventually, after challenging the story for a number of years, I began to teach workshops, speaking to hundreds and sometimes thousands of people a month. What happened to my shyness? I still have it, but now I also have the ability to be "not shy."

Likewise, you have undoubtedly developed, with the help of others, stories about yourself. Some of these stories—such as "I'm organized," or "I'm great with kids"—are fine; you like them and the results they help produce in your life. But some of them aren't so wonderful and don't help you solve problems or live a happier life. Another way to change the viewing, then, is to challenge unhelpful ideas that you have about yourself, your life, and your problem. I call this developing *solution-oriented life stories.*

There is a children's game that illustrates the idea of being blocked by unhelpful stories. A room is set up with chairs scattered throughout. One child agrees to attempt to walk through the room blindfolded without hitting any chairs, after first trying to memorize a clear pathway through the maze. After the child is blindfolded, the other children quietly move the chairs to the side of the room and then watch with amusement as the blindfolded child walks a crooked path trying to avoid nonexistent obstacles (PV Eckhart, *Reader's Digest,* Jan. 1994, p. 16).

Most of us have stories or beliefs in our lives that are like those chairs. We don't ask for a raise because we decide it is impossible. We are afraid we are not smart enough to go for that college degree. We don't ask someone we have a crush on out for a date, We don't submit our artwork, poetry, writing, or song to someone who might publish or buy it. We fear public speaking and avoid it like the plague—all because we have stories that are problem-oriented rather than solution-oriented.

RECOGNIZING PROBLEM STORIES

What stories and ideas do you have about yourself or your problems that hold you back or keep you doing the same thing over and over again? Let's look at four types of stories that hamper change: (1) blame stories, (2) impossibility stories, (3) invalidation stories, and (4) nonaccountability stories.

Type 1: Blame Stories

Blame stories involve deciding that someone is bad or wrong or that a person has bad intentions. We can believe these stories about ourselves or about others. I might decide that you are trying to control me or that you are selfish. This usually doesn't help me solve the problem we're having or enlist your cooperation in changing. Or I can decide that I am lazy, sick, or crazy. That usually doesn't motivate me or help me make changes.

Blame stories usually don't help you or anyone else. I'm not saying that you can't hold yourself and other people accountable for what you or they do. We'll discuss that shortly. But holding people accountable is different from blame. *Blaming* means judging who is bad or has bad intentions. Blame keeps you stuck in the past, focused on who or what messed you up or caused your current problems.

In *I'm Dysfunctional, You're Dysfunctional* (1992), Wendy Kaminer tells a poignant story of a discovery she made about survivors of trauma. In the course of writing a book about various self-help groups such as adult children of alcoholics or adults abused as children, she attended hundreds of meetings. In her view, most of the self-help meetings were characterized by self-pitying, blaming others, and endlessly revisiting traumatic childhood experiences. In the midst of her research, she visited a group of Cambodian women, survivors of the killing fields who had fled to this new and strange country, most of whom had experienced and seen untold horrors. Kaminer was struck by the contrast between the Cambodian women's group and the self-help groups she was researching. The Cambodian women spoke little about the past or blame and spent much of their time helping each other learn practical things that could help them in their everyday lives: more English phrases, the local bus system, and so on.

Type 2: Impossibility Stories

There's an old saying that summarizes this type of problem story: "If you decide something is impossible, you are right. If you decided that it's possible, you're also right!" Most of the progress that's been made in human history has been by people who did not accept that something was impossible. The rocket scientist Wernher von Braun said, "I have learned to use the word 'impossible' with the greatest caution." You'll find enough limitations in the world without telling yourself stories that limit you.

A series of experiments was done with dogs in the 1960s, in which the dogs were put into raised cages that had wire mesh bottoms. Each cage was divided into two chambers, separated by a barrier with a dog-sized hole cut in it. The experiment involved giving a mild electric shock on one side of the cage. Of course, the dogs would quickly move to the unshocked side of the cage. Then, the experimenters gave the shock on both sides of the cage. For a time, the dogs went back and forth from one side to the other, trying to escape the shock. When it became clear to them that there was no escape from the shock, the dogs lay down and stopped trying. They would no longer get up and try to move away from the shock. Then the experimenters turned off the shock in the other side of the cage, wondering when the dogs would discover that they could escape the discomfort. Most dogs never did. They had learned that escaping the shock was *impossible*, so why bother trying? This is an impossibility story.

Now, if you were paying close attention, you might have noticed that I wrote that *most* of the dogs never found out the shock was turned off in the other part of the cage. A few did. They persisted despite the evidence to the contrary and were able to escape the shock. The experimenters went on to do similar research with humans. (No, they didn't put them in wire cages and shock them!) They conducted tests to measure people's attitudes and explanations and found that certain people had an "impossibility" mind-set. They were thinking like the discouraged dogs in the cages. These people believed that they had no power to change anything and that problems were persistent, long-lasting, pervasive, and inescapable. This view became self-fulfilling. Since these people didn't take actions to change their unhappy situations, they had more problems in their lives.

A woman in her fifties came to see me for help with problems in her marriage. She complained that her husband wasn't very affectionate and she was dissatisfied with the marriage. When I asked her what kinds of things she would like her husband to do to show her more affection, she answered, "Well, my husband was raised in a family of five boys on an Iowa farm." I was at a loss to see how this was an answer to my question until she explained that she wanted her husband to hold her hand and put his arm around her, to express his affection for her in physical ways. But she had read that boys who were raised in families in which little to no physical affection was expressed were unable to express such affection as adults. Consequently, she had decided that her husband was incapable of showing affection. She was thinking in terms of impossibility. There was no way for her to get what she wanted in her marriage, and she was seriously considering leaving it to find a husband who had grown up in a different kind of family.

I told her that I thought perhaps her husband was capable of the kind of affection she longed for. Had he ever held her hand or put his arm around her? Yes, she remembered that when they were "sparking" (an old-fashioned term for courting or dating), he had often put his arm around her and they held hands constantly. I asked her if she thought that the muscles he used to reach out to her physically had atrophied in the ensuing years. She laughed and said, "Probably not." I agreed and told her that we were now going to work on getting him to be more physically affectionate.

If we decide that change is impossible, we often prevent ourselves and others from trying to make change happen.

Type 3: Invalidation Stories

Sometimes we decide that our own or someone else's feelings, thoughts, or self is wrong. We might think that others are oversensitive if their feelings are hurt by something we say or do. Or we might decide that what they are interested in is stupid or wrong.

I worked with a couple who had a persistent problem. The husband loved to fly his private plane. The wife thought that flying was a stupid, dangerous hobby and a waste of money. Every weekend when the weather was good, they went through an incredibly repetitive game with each other. Sometime on Sunday afternoon, the husband would casually get up from his easy chair, stretch, and say he was going out for a drive in the country. He would then sneak out to the airfield. His wife would get suspicious and go out to the airfield, angrily confronting him when he touched down—both for deceiving her and for wasting their money on his stupid hobby. She thought his interests were invalid, stupid, and wrong. Her stories about him were invalidating. Consequently, they were doomed to repeat this hurtful pattern.

Now, the husband in the example above was certainly wrong to deceive his wife. But when it comes to people's desires and core interests, there is no right or wrong—there are just different strokes for different folks. The problem comes when one person claims that the other person's different strokes are, in some way, not right.

In the early days of psychoanalysis, analysts were convinced that women who needed clitoral stimulation in order to have an orgasm were having "immature" orgasms. They communicated this interpretation to many women, who felt as if their desires and needs were wrong and strove to have "correct" desires and "mature" orgasms (requiring a penis in the vagina). By the time Masters and Johnson published the first laboratory studies showing that the female orgasm was clitoral, even when it involved insertion of the penis, untold numbers of women had bought an invalidating story about their sexuality.

Type 4: Nonaccountability Stories

It's all too easy these days to feel as if we are not responsible for what we do. The media have given us all sorts of excuses. We can blame it on genetics (*you were just born that way and can't help it*). Or we can blame it on a painful and difficult childhood (*you are an adult child of an alcoholic*). Or we can blame it on another person (*she or he made me do it*). Sometimes we get the idea that we don't have a choice or aren't accountable for our actions.

But that is simply a story. People have choices, not always about what they feel or think or about their biochemistry, but about what they do. We as humans have choices about the actions we take. You may feel like hitting or killing someone, but you do not have to act on that feeling. You may have a genetic predisposition to drink alcohol to excess, but your genes don't make you pick up a glass and drink. Your shopping addiction does not call QVC and order thousands of dollars worth of merchandise—*you* do.

Once I did marriage therapy with a couple who had separated. The husband had consistently betrayed his wife by indulging in affairs and excessive drinking and by running them into deep debt. When they finally separated, she had reestablished some basic credit under her own name. He had then stolen her credit card and charged it to the maximum while on a drinking binge. She asked me to meet with them so she could have some support when she told him of her decision to divorce him. Knowing what was coming, he got drunk before the meeting. When his wife told him of her intention, he began to cry and claimed that he had no power over his behavior, since he was an alcoholic. I suggested that "powerlessness," as defined by Alcoholics Anonymous, didn't mean this at all. It meant that since he had a genetic predisposition to drink and was powerless over alcohol once he started drinking, he should do what he could to avoid taking the first drink—and that he was still accountable for what he did while he was drinking.

Solution Key 6

CHANGE PROBLEM STORIES INTO SOLUTION STORIES

Luckily, we are not stuck with our problem stories. We can change them by challenging them. In my practice, I have found several effective ways to help people challenge their problem stories and start to develop stories that are more solution-oriented and more helpful.

FOUR TYPES OF PROBLEM STORIES

Type 1: **Blame stories**

These are stories in which someone, yourself or someone else, gets the blame—that is, gets pinned with bad traits (like "selfish," "crazy," or "oversensitive") or with bad intentions ("You only want to control me," or "I must want attention; that's why I have these problems"). Not only don't these stories invite change, but they can actively interfere with the change process.

Type 2: **Impossibility stories**

These stories hold that change is impossible in a given situation.

Type 3: **Invalidation stories**

These stories suggest that someone's feelings, desires, thoughts, or personality is somehow wrong or unacceptable.

Type 4: **Nonaccountability stories**

These stories excuse people from responsibility for their actions by claiming that they are under the control of genetic programming, other people, or some other factor that is beyond their control.

Changing Stories, Method 1: Acknowledge and Describe

One way to change stories is to move descriptions from the general to the specific, dropping theories, predictions, and explanations from your thinking. For example, instead of, "I'm depressed and I'll never feel better," one might just acknowledge, "I feel a certain tiredness in my muscles, I feel lethargic, and I have thoughts that say I'll never get better." Sometimes just examining, acknowledging, or speaking about our experience frees us from old interpretations and stories.

If the dogs in the experiment described earlier could have just acknowledged that *right now* there is no escape from the shock, they might have realized that at any moment in the future, there might be a time when the shock was no longer present. Their *experience* was not being able to escape the shock, but their story was that they would *never* be able to escape it.

Likewise, if the women in analysis had just stayed with their experience and acknowledged that they enjoyed and desired stimulation of their clitoral area and that this led to orgasms for them, they could have bypassed the invalidation and shame they felt for having the "wrong" kind of desire or orgasm.

Summary of Method 1

ACKNOWLEDGE AND DESCRIBE

Just *describe* a situation, rather than judge it.

Exercise 1: Acknowledge and Describe Problem Situations

1. Focus on some situation or person that is problematic for you. Write it down.
2. Acknowledge your feelings about that situation by writing them down.
3. Describe, as if you could see or hear a videotape, what happened or what happens in the upsetting situation. If it is a person, describle what (not why) the person does or did. Do not add any explanations or labels.

Changing Stories, Method 2: Find or Create Counterevidence

Problem stories are undermined when you find counterevidence in your life that doesn't fit with the story. Or you can act in a way that challenges a story directly. When I started to act in ways that didn't fit with my story about myself as "shy," I found myself believing it less and less.

A woman who was due to come in with her husband for marriage therapy in a few weeks decided to visit the counselor early and tell her side of things. She told the counselor that she wanted a divorce and had agreed to counseling only to assuage her husband's anxiety. She knew that the marriage was over because he was, in her words, a "wimp." He didn't have the guts (she actually used a cruder term) to stand up to her or even stay in the same room during an argument. He was terrified that she would leave him. He would do anything to placate her when she got upset. He would run around the house and clean it while she was at work. He would get their children to clean their rooms. He would often try to stop an argument by giving his wife a little dessert treat he had secretly baked for her while she was at work. (I know some of the women reading this book will want this man's phone number.) She longed for a man who would stand up to her, who was willing to fight it out and not be such a wimp. She was certain her husband could never be such a man, and she wanted the counselor to know that she intended to divorce him.

She went home and told her husband about her intention. As you might imagine, he pleaded for her to reconsider. He called the counselor in a panic, asking for ideas about what he could do to change his wife's mind. "She's got you stereotyped as a wimp," the counselor told him. "I know," he replied weakly. "The only advice I can give you is to act in ways that will blow her image of you between now and the time you both come in for counseling together," the counselor suggested. The husband agreed to give it a try.

When they arrived for their counseling session several weeks later, they related the following story. One evening they had begun to argue about something. As usual, the husband was trying to avoid the argument and placate his wife. Finally, he asked her to just be quiet for a minute and close her eyes. He had a surprise for her. As she expected, he appeared from the kitchen in a few minutes with a banana cream pie. Then he threw the pie right into her face.

She sat dumbfounded for a minute and then began to laugh, and so did he. She told the counselor that she never imagined he would have the guts to do anything that might upset her like that and, as a result, she had some real hope that maybe the marriage could change. Before, she had considered him to be a wimp—born a wimp, genetically programmed to live as a wimp and die as a wimp. Now she began to see that he was doing wimpy things and he could change that. Obviously, she didn't really want pies thrown in her face, and the counselor began to work with the couple on what she did want and what would persuade her to stay in the marriage. During the next week, at the wife's request, the couple had an argument in which the husband promised not to try to calm her down or keep the peace in any way. He also promised to stand toe-to-toe with his wife during the argument, which he found very challenging, but *possible.*

A friend of mine grew up knowing that she had been adopted after being given up in infancy by her biological mother. She was told that she had been in five different foster homes during her crucial early months, when bonding and attachment occur. When she had problems in relationships in her adult life, she decided that she must have "abandonment issues" and that these were preventing her from having fulfilling relationships. Many years later, she contacted her biological mother, who gave her quite a different account of her early life. Her biological mother had visited her often while she was in foster care, and had fed her, talked to her, and tried to find a way to keep her. In the end, the mother, who was very young, succumbed to pressure from her own parents and the adoption agency and reluctantly agreed to the adoption. Upon hearing this new account, my friend said, she felt as if gears were grinding in her brain, as her story about being an abandoned, unwanted orphan deprived of early bonding fell apart.

Summary of Method 2

FIND OR CREATE COUNTEREVIDENCE

Find evidence that doesn't fit in with a story, or challenge the story directly.

Exercise 2: Challenge Your Problem Stories

Write down any stories you believe about yourself or your current problem. You may have to talk with a friend in order to help yourself identify these stories. It is sometimes hard to clarify stories on our own, since we have lived with them and believed them for so long.

For example, your story may be that you are dumb and can't learn new things. Or it may be that you are bad because you were sexually abused or are divorced.

Next, make a list of any evidence that would challenge or contradict those stories.

To challenge the stories above, you could remind yourself that you did learn to rollerblade last year and that you know the names of all the state capitals—or that you have friends who were sexually abused or divorced but who you think are good people.

Changing Stories, Method 3: Realize That You Are Not Your Story

People often become so identified with their problems that they begin to think of themselves as the problem. Other people can reinforce this process. Therapists and doctors often use shorthand to refer to their clients or patients: *I have several depressives in my practice,* or *I specialize in treating diabetics.* This shorthand can sometimes turn a story into a label that sticks. Of course, people are not just depressives or diabetics; a person may also be a teacher, a father, a mother, a brother, a mechanic, a doctor, a fisherman, nice, funny, and so on.

Earlier in this chapter, I described how I began to challenge my story of being "shy." I realized that shyness wasn't a fixed state that would define me for the rest of my days. Later in my life, I did the same thing with "depression." I began to think that perhaps I was "doing" depression rather than that I was "depressive." That helped me find the freedom to start doing "not depressive" things, and I found out that doing those things helped me to become less depressed.

Summary of Method 3

REALIZE THAT YOU ARE NOT YOUR STORY

Challenge and change your label. Remind yourself that you are more than just your story.

Exercise 3: Challenge and Change Your Label

Write down any unhelpful labels that you have pinned yourself with or that have been pinned on you by others.

For example, you may have gotten a reputation for being impulsive.

Now write down all the qualities you have that remind you that you are not totally defined by the unhelpful or unflattering labels.

To challenge the story about you in the example above, you could write down that you are loyal and stick with people through thick and thin. You could also write down that you do careful research before making large purchases.

Changing Stories, Method 4: Create Compassionate and Helpful Stories

This section offers a selection of more helpful stories that you can tell yourself about yourself, your problem situations, and other people—stories that have compassion and possibilities built into them.

One of the most common words in the invalidating, self-blaming stories we believe about ourselves or our situations is the word *should*. The psychologist Albert Ellis has coined the phrase *Stop shoulding on yourself.* When you tell yourself that you should feel or be another way, you are likely to feel bad about yourself.

As an alternative, try telling yourself that it is okay to feel or be the way you are, even though you have some idea that you should feel or be different.

A therapist friend of mine had a client who couldn't stop crying during her first session. Finally, he was able to understand a bit of the problem that she was gasping out between sobs: "It's my horse," she said.

"What about your horse?" he asked.

"He died," she sobbed.

"Oh, I'm sorry," he replied.

"Yes, but he died two years ago and I can't stop grieving for him. I miss him so. My husband tells me I should be over this by now. My friends tell me it is silly to still grieve for a horse. My doctor tried to give me tranquilizers to get me to stop being so upset. But I can't seem to stop."

"Well, who made the rule that you must stop grieving in two years?" my friend asked. "It's okay to grieve as long as you grieve, whether it is for a horse or a person. We all have a different way of grieving and a different schedule for doing so. No one knows what's right for anyone else."

The woman stopped crying and looked up in amazement, "You mean it's okay to grieve for my horse?"

"Yes, that is what I am saying," my friend replied.

"Thank you. Would you like to see pictures of the horse?"

"Certainly," said my friend.

With that, they spent the rest of the time looking at the pictures while the woman reminisced about the horse and the very special relationship they had. She shed a few tears, but nothing like the convulsive sobbing she had been doing at home and earlier in the session. She reported at the next therapy session that she had told her friends and her husband that she had a perfect right to grieve and intended to do so as long as she needed. She also said that she had been crying much less and feeling some moments of peace about the loss. The point is not that she couldn't have done something to change her grief, but that she was being invalidated for feeling grief and that it was her decision when to adopt nongrieving behaviors and move on.

It's important to be gentle with yourself about your feelings and who you are. If you get down on yourself for having diabetes or having a tendency toward depression, it won't help you deal with your situation any better and will probably make things worse. The same holds true for your view of others.

While I was growing up, my father would often slip me a five-dollar bill and say, "Here's five dollars—don't tell your mom." My mom thought that my father was too generous with money. As I thought about this later in life, I realized that this was his way of saying, "I love you." I, like most people, preferred to get my love directly with the words "I love you" and a hug. But I also realized

Solution Key 6

CHANGE PROBLEM STORIES INTO SOLUTION STORIES

Method 1: **Acknowledge and describe.**
Instead of evaluating, judging, or explaining the situation, just acknowledge your experience and the facts of the situation, describing it rather than characterizing it.

Method 2: **Find or create counterevidence.**
Find some evidence that contradicts the unhelpful story.

Method 3: **Realize that you are not your story.**
Remind yourself that whatever story you have is not all there is to you.

Method 4: **Create compassionate and helpful stories.**
Find a kinder, gentler view of yourself, someone else, or your situation.

that this was my father's way of expressing his love. After this realization, every time my father slipped me some money (he never broke this habit) and said, "Don't tell your mother," I would mentally translate that into, "I love you, son."

When my father first became ill with cancer, I called him on the phone. When the conversation came to a close, I said, "I just want you to know how much I appreciate all you've done for me as a father. I love you, Dad." My father quickly replied, "Yeah, I love all you kids." I just shrugged and again realized my father's discomfort with any direct expressions of love.

In the third and final year of my father's fight against cancer, he came to stay in Arizona, where I was going to college; but after a short time he became so ill that he had to return to Nebraska. As I was sitting with him in the departure lounge at the airport, we both knew that this was probably the last time we would see each other. I turned to him and said, "I love you, Dad." My father looked away and said, "Well, I love all you kids." While I looked into my father's eyes, I repeated very slowly, "No, Dad, I want to make sure you hear me. *I love you.*" My father started to cry, we hugged, and he whispered, "I love you."

My father finally acted in accord with my way of perceiving love; yet even if he had never said, "I love you," I still would have known that he loved me. I understood that "Here's five dollars—don't tell your mom" was love, too. Instead of criticizing his limitations, I felt compassion for his way of expressing himself and how unused he was to direct expressions of love and affection, a pattern he had learned from both his family and his culture. To have compassion and accept my father, I had to stop telling myself the negative story that he *should* be able to say he loved me or that he was too cold or emotionally insecure to say it.

In the middle of an argument, if you can begin to imagine how the other person really sees the situation and how he or she is feeling at that moment, and if you have compassion, you will be likely to soften and speak more kindly.

Summary of Method 4

CREATE COMPASSIONATE AND HELPFUL STORIES

Tell yourself stories about yourself, your problems, and others that have compassion and possibilities built in.

Exercise 3: Find a Compassionate Story

The next time you find yourself getting angry with or down on yourself for being who you are or feeling what you are feeling, imagine that a loving and compassionate friend is talking to you about what you are feeling or how you are. What would this friend say during his or her most compassionate moments?

If you are a religious or spiritually oriented person, you might also imagine that a spiritual figure or force (like Jesus, Allah, Buddha, the Holy Spirit, cosmic Consciousness, or the universe) is visiting you. Imagine what message this figure would give you. What story or view would this figure have of you or your situation? What comforting or compassionate advice or message would there be for you?

This last idea is a nice segue into the solution key we'll be exploring in Chapter 8: using solution-oriented spirituality to resolve your problems.

CHAPTER 8

RISING ABOVE YOURSELF

Solution-Oriented Spirituality

> Sometimes I go about pitying myself, and all along, my soul is being blown by great winds across the sky.
>
> —Ojibway saying

I once read a story in which a man said that he had become spiritual when his father died. Up until that time in his life, he had been able to deal with everything that had happened to him as a person. But for some reason, handling his father's death had been beyond him. He couldn't seem to deal with the loss, the grief, and the overwhelming feeling that he would never be okay again. After a while he realized that since he couldn't deal with it, the only way he would be able to go on was to draw on what was beyond him: spirituality.

Spirituality is what is beyond the individual personality. It goes by many different names and can be accessed in many different ways. Some call it the soul, some God, some Allah, some Jehovah, some the higher self, some the universe, some nature; but all these refer to something that is beyond the little isolated ego we sometimes feel ourselves to be.

I heard a story about a woman who grew up in Texas. When she was having trouble in her life, she would visit her grandmother, who lived nearby and always had a kind word and some wisdom to pass on. One day she was complaining to her grandmother about some situation and her grandmother just turned to her, smiled sadly, and said, "Sometimes, darlin', you've just got to rise above yourself in this life." I've remembered that wise advice many times as I have faced trouble in my life. Spirituality is another way of saying, "Rise above yourself."

In this chapter, we will look at a particular approach to accessing and using spirituality to help you deal with and resolve problems: solution-oriented spirituality.

Solution Key 7

USE SPIRITUALITY TO TRANSCEND OR RESOLVE PROBLEMS

Spirituality, Method 1: Find Your Pathway to Spirituality

Spirituality refers to what is beyond the "little self," or the personality. Anything that gives one an experience of the "bigger self," or what is beyond the limited personality, can be a component of spirituality. If the word *spirituality* turns you off or has negative connotations, just think of this as anything that pulls you out of your limited day-to-day view and gives you a sense of connection with something beyond yourself. The seven pathways listed below are possible avenues for people to connect with that "something beyond." Any one may work. Some may not work for you or may not appeal to you. Some you may have used before. If you haven't accessed spirituality in one of these ways, pick one that appeals to you—or more than one—and give it a try.

Pathway 1: Connect to the Soul, the Deeper Self

This pathway involves going to the deepest level within—referred to as soul, inner wisdom, the unconscious, or intuition. This is the level of one's relationship with oneself. People enter into this level through meditation, contemplation, or some other means of listening deeply to one's inner life. In the hubbub and noise of everyday life, most people can't hear the soul. Silence and contemplation seem to be necessary for most people to connect with their soul.

Pathway 2: Connect Through the Body

Various spiritual and religious traditions use body movement to access spirituality. I was in the Caribbean once and went into a supermarket. The woman who was ringing up my groceries was carrying on a conversation with the checker next to her. "What church do you go to?" she asked her coworker. "The Presbyterian church," the other replied. "Oh, I couldn't go there," my checker said, shaking her upper body and waving her arms, "I go to the Baptist. I need to *move* to find God." Some people find that dancing, sex, athletics, eating fine foods, chanting, yoga, or other body activities connect them to a sense of what is beyond them.

One of my favorite poems—*Wild Geese*, by Mary Oliver—speaks to this pathway:

> You do not have to be good. . . . You only have to let the
> soft animal of your body love what it loves.

I treasure that image: *the soft animal of your body*. You only have to let the soft animal of your body love what it loves. This speaks powerfully of going through the body to find spirituality and connection.

Pathway 3: Connect to Another

Sometimes in our connection with another—a child, a friend, a spouse, even a stranger encountered by chance—we find the means to transcend our own petty concerns and feel a sense of connection with something beyond ourselves. I am referring here to intimate one-to-one relationships. The theologian and philosopher Martin Buber called these *I-thou* relationships. In these I-thou connections, as opposed to the typical encounters we have with one another, we actually experience the full sense of the other person—not just a cartoon or a caricature of who we think the person is, and not just as an object to fulfill our needs.

I remember when my son Patrick was born. I felt as though a fire hose of love was opened up in my heart and was pouring love toward him. I knew in that instant that, if it ever came to it, I would die for him. In that relationship, I had effortlessly transcended my own concerns.

I had a client I had been seeing for some time who had been severely sexually abused when she was a young child. I had come to admire her courage and persistence in dealing with this difficult life she had had, and to care for her a great deal. She, however, was very self-critical, always judging herself very harshly for any little mistake she made. She felt that she was a bad person and generally unacceptable. As she sat talking to me about what a terrible person she was, I began to tear up as I saw what a truly good person she was and that she didn't recognize it. She stopped as she saw my tears, "What is it?" she asked, genuinely concerned for me. I told her that if she could only see herself through my eyes for a moment, she would never say those terrible things she was saying about herself. She was a bit stunned, and we sat in silence for a few minutes as the tears in my eyes began to be mirrored by tears in hers. Several weeks later, she told me that she had, for that one instant, seen herself through my eyes. In that moment, she had caught a glimpse of the possibility that maybe she wasn't such a bad person—perhaps even that she was a good and lovable person. After that moment, much as her old self-critical habits tried to reestablish themselves, something deep within her no longer believed that she was so terrible.

Pathway 4: Connect to Community and a Contribution to the World

Most people find spirituality through worship in a group or community of like-minded people. Feeling connected to a group can give one a sense of connection to something greater than oneself.

A young woman had been in and out of psychiatric hospitals for depression and suicidal impulses. Each time she was in the hospital, she would become much less depressed and her suicidal impulses would abate. Finally, after her third hospitalization, one of the staff members noticed the pattern and asked the young woman about why she thought she did so much better in the hospital. "Because I am not so isolated. When I am alone, my depressive thoughts can take over and I don't have a sense that anyone cares whether I am dead or alive. When I am here, I know that people care for me and I am not so isolated." The staff member arranged for the hospital chaplain to visit the young woman and invite her to visit his congregation, which was a vibrant church with many activities for young people. She became involved in the church and never returned to the hospital.

Sometimes committing to causes greater than oneself that contribute to the community or the planet gives people the same sense of uplift and serenity. The poet Rainer Maria Rilke says, "If I don't manage to fly, someone else will. The spirit wants only that there be flying. As for who happens to do it, in that he has only a passing interest." Some people, like Mother Teresa, feel called to a great mission to contribute to others. They have the sense that spirit has chosen them to fly.

Pathway 5: Connect to the Earth or Nature

Some people find that being in nature connects them with a sense of transcendence and renewal. Research has shown that when workers have a view of nature from their offices, they are typically more productive. Is nature a way that you connect with your spirituality or regain a sense of purpose and perspective?

A man was burned out in his career. He had been going to school to pursue an advanced degree while working full time, as well as raising two children with his wife. When he realized that he had made a commitment to be one of the chaperones on his son's camping trip in the wilderness for two weeks, he groaned at the thought of more responsibility and activity. But, he figured, at least he would get some time away from work.

The first day was difficult. His mind was on work and on all his responsibilities. But by the end of the first week, he was feeling renewed and energetic, even though the days had been filled with vigorous physical activities and he was terribly out of shape. Being in nature and using his body left him invigorated.

By the end of the two weeks, he vowed that he would arrange to spend at least one day a month hiking in nature. He followed through on this plan and was able to complete his degree without feeling so overwhelmed and burned out.

Pathway 6: Participate in Making or Appreciating Art

Have you ever seen people carried away by art? They stand in the art museum, crying while looking at a painting. Or they listen to an opera, enraptured and transported. Literature, painting, sculpture, theater, movies, photography, dance, and music have long been avenues for people to transcend their day-to-day lives and be transported or transformed. One can be transported either while creating art or while observing an artist's performance or product.

Several movies detail how prisoners in terrible, torturous circumstances have transcended and survived their situations by playing in a prison camp orchestra or singing in a choir. Art can lift us out of our present circumstances to another realm.

Pathway 7: Connect to God or a Higher Power

I read a story about the origins of Alcoholics Anonymous (AA). Before AA was founded, an acquaintance of one of its founders was in treatment with the eminent psychiatrist Carl Jung. This man, who was a chronic, episodic binge drinker, greatly admired Jung's guidance and wisdom. But after going on yet another drinking binge, he made another appointment with Jung and asked desperately if there weren't some way that Jung could help him to stop this terrible drinking pattern. It was ruining his life; and even though he wanted to stop, he found that he couldn't. Jung shook his head and told him that he had never been able to cure anyone who was so seriously addicted to alcohol. In fact, Jung said, he was not aware that psychotherapy had ever cured such an advanced case. As you might imagine, the man was devastated to hear that the great Carl Jung could offer no encouragement or hope. "Isn't there anything that would help?" he pleaded. "Well," Jung replied, "the only thing I've ever seen help people in your condition is being converted to a deep belief in God." *Great*, the man thought, *how is that going to help me?* He asked what Jung would do in his place. "I would go to every religious revival meeting I could find and hope that one of them took," recommended Jung. In fact, that is just what the man did. He ended up being converted during a meeting of the Oxford Group, a Christian revivalist movement that was popular earlier in the twentieth century. Out of that experience came the famous step in the AA twelve-step program that involves surrendering to a "higher power" as a crucial part of the pathway to sobriety.

This pathway, then, involves connecting to the universe, or a higher power, or God in a powerful, experiential (not just intellectual) way. There are many means of connecting this way; and once you begin to focus on this pathway, you will see people doing it in different ways all around you.

Summary of Method 1

FIND YOUR PATHWAY TO SPIRITUALITY

Connect to the soul, the body, another person, the community, nature, art, or a higher power.

Spirituality, Method 2:
Access Your Spirituality Using the Past, Present, or Future

You can search in the past, the present, and the future for spiritual solutions and resources to help you with a current problem.

Access Through the Past: Remembering Past Spiritual Experiences and Connections

In Chapter 2, we explored the idea that one of the most effective ways to solve problems is to recall previous times when things went well or when you solved problems, and reuse those skills. You can apply the same general idea to reaccess your sense of spirituality. Here are some questions to facilitate your search for solutions in the past:

- Have you ever had religious or spiritual beliefs or followed religious or spiritual practices?

- Have those been helpful in any way?
- Have you ever felt connected to something more than yourself, such as nature, humanity, the universe, or God?
- What, if anything, has been your most profound spiritual experience?

Access Through the Present: Recognize Present Spiritual Resources and Solutions

Now search in your present life for ways to access spirituality. Here are some questions that might help focus your search:

- What do you do or where do you go to recharge your batteries when you get a chance?
- Do you attend religious services? If so, what is the best feeling you get from these services?
- What kind of artistic activities do you enjoy?
- How do you connect with other people?
- Do you think you have a purpose for being alive? If so, what is it?
- Is there any religious or spiritual figure or activity that you think would be helpful to you in this situation?

Access Through the Future: Create Future Spiritual Hopes and Intentions

If you haven't found ways to access spirituality in the past or the present, you can always use the future to create some new possibilities in the present. Ask yourself these and similar questions to create a compelling vision of where you'd like to be spiritually in the future:

- What kind of spiritual or religious activities would you like to do in the future, if any?

- Is there any area of your inner or spiritual life you would like to develop more?
- Is there any spiritual or religious figure that you would like to use as a model for you? In what way?

Summary of Method 2

ACCESS YOUR SPIRITUALITY USING THE PAST, PRESENT, OR FUTURE

Search the past, present, and future for spiritual solutions and resources to help with a current problem.

Spirituality, Method 3: Develop Compassion, Service, and Faith

Evoke and Connect with Compassion for Others and Yourself

The ideals of compassion and service are fundamental to most religious and spiritual traditions. My dictionary defines compassion as "the deep feeling of sharing the suffering of another, together with the inclination to give aid or support or to show mercy." Most of the time, we are judging or evaluating others; but the great spiritual figures whom most of us admire, such as Jesus, Buddha, Martin Luther King, Jr., and Mahatma Gandhi, were accepting and nonjudgmental. Jesus embraced lepers and prostitutes. Gandhi touched the "untouchables."

When we endure our own tragedies or trials, most of us develop some empathy and compassion for others who are suffering. The trick is to keep that sense of compassion going throughout our daily lives, when we are likely to go on automatic pilot and move back into being judgmental—especially when times are tough.

Exercise 1: Connecting with Compassion

Of course, I have a solution-oriented exercise for you. Recall a time when you were most in need of understanding and compassion. How would you have wanted others to speak to you? How would you have wanted them to relate to you? What words or what tone of voice would have been most comforting and helpful to you at that time? What actions would have made a difference? Perhaps someone offered you some kindness, understanding, or compassion during that time. What did that person do?

Now think about how you could apply what you have remembered to someone around you who needs compassion at this moment. It could be your boss, your child, your spouse, a friend, or someone you don't even know.

Of course, as I wrote in Chapter 7, this sense of compassion can be applied to yourself as well. If you are suffering, how could you bring that sense of compassion into your life for what you are suffering right now? What kinds of merciful, accepting, nonjudgmental words, phrases, or actions could you use with yourself instead of your usual harsh judgment or self-criticism?

Service

> This is the true joy in life, the being used up for a purpose recognized by yourself as a mighty one; the being a force of nature instead of a feverish, selfish little clod of ailments and grievances, complaining that the world will not devote itself to making you happy. I am of the opinion that my life belongs to the community, and as long as I live, it is my privilege to do for it whatever I can. I want to be thoroughly used up when I die, for

> the harder I work the more I live. I rejoice in life for its own sake. Life is no "brief candle" to me. It is a sort of splendid torch which I have got hold of for a moment, and I want to make it burn as brightly as possible before handing it on to future generations.
>
> —George Bernard Shaw

As I was writing this book, my wife was suffering from a serious and potentially fatal illness. I grew up in a house where the unwritten rule was: Don't get sick. My mother was a strong farm girl with great midwestern work values. Unless you were unable, you got up every day and went to work or school, even with a fever or a sore throat. When we kids got sick, she would let us stay home only if we were so sick we couldn't get out of bed. And if we were sick at home, we were to stay in bed, not watch television or read or do anything that was fun. You really had to be sick to face that kind of boredom. She would leave us alone to heal, sticking her head into the bedroom every few hours to see if we needed anything to drink or eat. But our job was to get better, so she left us to it.

When I grew up, I rarely got ill; and when I did, I wanted to be left alone to be sick until I got better. I treated my partners the same way. Some of them had grown up in different kinds of families and were quite upset that I left them all alone when they were sick. I was pretty unsympathetic. My thinking, unkind as it may seem, was shaped by my childhood experiences. "Your job is to get well. Don't be a wimp. You shouldn't be rewarded for being sick, or it will get to be a habit for you."

So, when my wife grew so deathly ill that she needed to have all her food cooked by me, and I had to do all the household chores, pay the bills, and handle other duties in addition to earning the family income, I was wondering how I would manage, given my family conditioning. I had to wake up from a deep sleep in the middle of the night to take her to the bathroom when she was too weak to go by herself. I cleaned up after her when she vomited or dropped her food or drink. I had to soothe her when she was afraid that she would never get better, and comfort her when her body was racked with pain.

I found that I could do this willingly and lovingly when I entered into it with an attitude of service. It became a discipline of love and kindness that I think benefited me as much as it did her. It was very humbling to do the mundane duties of caring for my wife and the household. I felt very grateful for the opportunity to be of service and make a contribution to someone who was suffering so and whom I loved. I "rose above myself" and my childhood programming.

This is the paradoxical effect of service: those who do service often get as much benefit as those who are served, or more. Also paradoxically, you can't go into the performance of the service with the motive of getting personal benefit out of it; you must enter into it purely altruistically. Only then do you reap its profound personal rewards.

Exercise 2: Doing Service

Anytime you find yourself troubled by some recurrent problem in your life, begin to make a plan to do some service for someone in your life or community who needs help or companionship. The next time the problem occurs, commit to spending as much time doing this service as you used to spend on the problem.

Faith

> Courage is not the towering oak that sees storms come and go; it is the fragile blossom that opens in the snow.
>
> —Alice Mackenzie Swain

The poet David Whyte talks about faith during difficult times in our lives, as having trust in the idea that the darkness will pass and there will again be light. He jokes that it would be silly if we decided to stop our lives when the moon was waning and the nights got darker and darker. If a friend called us up, we would say, "Sorry, but I don't do anything while the moon is fading. We'll have to wait until it is starts getting full again." Faith is trusting, when things look dark, that everything is not hopeless and lost forever. Keeping faith means making the commitment to keep moving through difficult times.

In the movie *Indiana Jones and the Last Crusade*, there is a scene in which Indy is following directions from an ancient guidebook for how to get to the Holy Grail. The directions are full of riddles and the path is fraught with danger, but as usual Indy barely escapes death and avoids all the traps—until the final clue. He knows that the Grail is across a chasm that is too wide for him to jump. It is miles down to the bottom of this canyon, but the instructions tell him to have faith and walk toward the Grail, and God will take care of him. No way is Indy going to do it, but he can't go back without the Grail. He closes his eyes and steps off, drops a short way, and stops, shocked that he didn't fall into the canyon. After he crosses the chasm he picks up some pebbles and throws them in the open space behind him. When they land, they reveal a hidden bridge that is disguised to blend in with the appearance of the chasm. Indy then goes on to obtain the Grail.

Faith is stepping out into the chasm when all evidence points to hopelessness. It is trusting that one can come out the other side of whatever one is in the middle of. "This too shall pass," goes the ancient wisdom. Gladys Taber writes in her book *Stillmeadow Road*: "People have seasons too, I think. There is something steadfast about people who withstand the chilling winds of trouble, the storms that assail the heart, and have the endurance and character to wait quietly for an April time."

Solution Key 7

USE SPIRITUALITY TO TRANSCEND OR RESOLVE PROBLEMS

Method 1: **Find your pathway to spirituality.**

Pathway 1: Connect to the soul, the deeper self.

Pathway 2: Connect through the body.

Pathway 3: Connect to another.

Pathway 4: Connect to community and a contribution to the world.

Pathway 5: Connect to the earth or nature.

Pathway 6: Participate in making or appreciating art.

Pathway 7: Connect to God or a higher power.

Method 2: **Access your spirituality using the past, present, or future.**

Remember past spiritual experiences and connections.
Recognize present spiritual resources and solutions.
Create future spiritual hopes and intentions.

Method 3: **Develop compassion, service, and faith.**

Summary of Method 3

DEVELOP COMPASSION, SERVICE, AND FAITH

Evoke and connect with compassion for others and yourself; perform service purely altruistically; and keep faith by making a commitment to keep moving through difficult times.

Exercise 3: Connecting with Faith

Recall a time when all seemed hopeless or you were panicky about some terrible news or some terrible development in your life, but things turned out better in the end than you expected. You made it through, or what you thought was terrible wasn't quite as terrible as you first imagined, or things were terrible but you learned something or developed in a direction that eventually was better for you.

Remind yourself of that past experience and work on developing faith in whatever problem situation you are now facing.

PART 3

APPLYING SOLUTION-ORIENTED THERAPY TO SPECIFIC AREAS OF YOUR LIFE

In Chapters 9 to 12, you will get some ideas about how to apply the solution-oriented approach to specific areas of your life: relationships, sex, and any unfinished issues that are affecting you in your current situation.

CHAPTER 9

THE CODEPENDENT CINDERELLA WHO LOVES A MAN WHO HATES WOMEN TOO MUCH

Solution-Oriented Relationships

> We have only one person to blame, and that's each other.
>
> —Barry Beck, New York Ranger, on who started a brawl during the NHL's Stanley Cup playoffs

When the guest at the family gathering found out that a therapist was present, she quickly cornered her and began to describe her marriage problems. "He's an alcoholic and a man who hates women. I'm an adult child of an alcoholic and a codependent. We fight all the time. What do you think will help us?" The therapist smiled, a bit overwhelmed by the litany of problems, which sounded as if they came from a list of titles in the self-help section of the bookstore, and replied, "I've been thinking about writing a book called *Women Who Read Too Much.*" The woman laughed and replied, "I'd probably read that one, too!"

ANALYSIS, BLAME, AND VAGUE TALK AS SOURCES OF RELATIONSHIP PROBLEMS

When relationships are in trouble, most of us have a tendency to analyze what is wrong with them. Unfortunately, the analysis usually shows that the other person has the problem.This typically produces a cycle of mutual recrimination, blame, and misunderstanding.

I do a lot of marriage counseling (my degree included a specialization in marriage and family therapy). I remember when the book *Men Who Hate Women and the Women Who Love Them* was first published. A couple would arrive at my office. The woman would tell me that she had read the book and had found it very eye-opening and validating. This was her relationship. Then she had given or shown the book to her husband, suggesting that he read it to gain insight into their problem (read: *his* problem). Predictably, he wouldn't be moved in a positive way by the book. He would either get angry, make fun of the book, or just ignore it. She would then be certain that her diagnosis was correct: he *was* a man who hated women. In the meantime, the relationship had not improved one whit and had usually deteriorated another notch.

The problem with analysis as an approach to resolving relationship difficulties, as we have discussed in the previous chapters, is that most of the time it doesn't really create solutions. It leads to explanations or stories about what is wrong, but it does not create love, restore lost intimacy, or resolve chronic arguing. Figuring out which planets you and your partner are from doesn't always help you down here on Earth.

In solution-oriented therapy, we use a different approach. You can apply these principles to your romantic and sexual relationships, your family life, your work life, your business, and your friends.

ACKNOWLEDGMENT REVISITED

After doing marriage counseling for over twenty-four years, I can tell you that many disagreements that I have witnessed and heard about in marriage and relationships could be bypassed if either person or both people in the relationship would just stop and acknowledge the other person's feelings and point of view. That doesn't mean that you have to agree with the other person or decide that he or she is right. It just means that you be able to comprehend and not dismiss the other person's sense of things.

A couple consulted me over the phone. I had seen the man before for individual work and for previous couples work with another partner. The couple were engaged to be married, but the man kept getting frightened and backing off from setting a wedding date. When he would express his doubts, his fiancée would react, and then they would be off to the races. I had seen this pattern in the previous relationship, so after ascertaining that in his clearest moments, the man truly did want to get married and that he loved his fiancée, I asked to speak with the woman alone. I told her that her partner was having doubts, so she could really help the situation if she just maintained confidence and calm in the face of his doubts and fears. All she had to do was listen and acknowledge her fiancé's fears. She didn't need to react to them. She responded that if she knew he wasn't seriously intending to leave the relationship, she would find it easy to do her part to keep things on an even keel. After this brief consultation, she was able to keep the bigger picture in mind even when her partner couldn't and was able to transcend her initial angry reaction for the good of the relationship. After a few more incidents when the man got scared and the woman just remained calm and listened to his doubts and fears, those fears diminished and they were able to set a wedding date. They remain happily married now, six years later.

Sometimes when you stop and listen without judging or rebutting, you'll find that you don't really have a problem with what the other person is saying or experiencing. You had been projecting some other meaning onto what he or she was saying or doing. Or you had reacted to your own story or interpretation about the implications of what was said or done.

Tom and John were friends who often went to baseball games together. One day Tom asked, "Why do we always have to go to baseball games? I'm getting tired of going to so many games." John immediately got upset and said that he could certainly find someone else to go with him if Tom didn't want to go. Tom was bewildered by John's anger. "Of course you could find someone else to go with you," he told John, "but I was thinking that we don't get enough time to talk at games. I have some problems at home and there is no chance to talk them over with you during the game because there are too many people who could overhear us and you seem so into the game that I don't want to distract you." John had believed a story—that Tom no longer wanted to spend time with him—but once he understood that Tom was asking for time to talk, he got less defensive. He had not really heard or understood what his friend was saying.

Sometimes after you acknowledge—by letting others know you have heard them and that they aren't crazy, bad, or wrong for feeling, thinking, or being as they are—you still have problems with what the other person is communicating. But then, at least the other person knows that you have heard and that the conflict is about what it is about rather than about not being heard or listened to.

In any case, it is crucial not to invalidate the other person. That is, do not give others the message that the way they see things or the way they are or feel is bad, wrong, or not valid in some way. If you invalidate, you are almost guaranteed a troublesome response from the other person.

Grace was a software designer for a high-tech firm. One day, during a staff meeting, she brought up an idea for a new product that the company could design. Her boss laughed and said, “So, who’s going to finance this fantasy blockbuster? You?” That day, tired of being invalidated and belittled, Grace called a headhunter who had been pursuing her and soon got another job. She went on to develop the product at the new company, and it did quite well in the marketplace.

When you think about it, you can see that these principles can be used successfully in many other interpersonal situations. The essence of good customer service starts with acknowledging the customer’s concerns. Good friendship relies on an ability to listen nonjudgmentally. Families work best when everyone’s feelings and points of views are heard and allowed. Often you are applying these principles in one area of your life, but not in another. You may be using them effectively at work, for example, but not as effectively at home.

Acknowledging and respectfully hearing the other person is only the first part of the formula for relating successfully to others. Next, we have to learn to adjust to one another and to change what we do with one another. This part of relationships is fraught with difficulties for most people. The next section, then, will give you some simple skills for talking to others about changes you want without getting mired in blame and misunderstanding.

ACTION TALK AS AN ANTIDOTE TO RELATIONSHIP PROBLEMS

Suppose you arrived at work one day and your boss confronted you and said, "You are messing up. I don't like your attitude, and if you don't change it, you'll be out of a job!" You might be shocked, but, more relevantly, would you know what to do to change your "attitude"? Probably not—especially if you thought your attitude was fine. You might start grousing to your coworkers or call your friends or family on the phone and tell them how terrible and unreasonable your boss is and what an awful place to work this is.

It would be much different if your boss confronted you and said, "The workday starts at 9 A.M. here. You have arrived at 9:30 the past few days. If you come in later than 9:05 A.M. any day for the next month, you will be fired." You might not like what your boss said, but at least you would know what you had to do to keep your job.

The point is that it is easier both to understand what someone else is unhappy about and to change it when you use *action talk*—that is, when you talk in a way that describes what someone has done or is doing or what you want him or her to do in the future. This bypasses the two typical communication problems in relationships: blame and vagueness.

Blame usually focuses on the bad qualities or the bad intentions that the other person has. Unfortunately, it is difficult to change qualities or intentions. Are you supposed to get a personality-ectomy? How are you going to change your intentions?

If you tell your husband or boyfriend that he is a man who hates women, how is he supposed to change that (provided that he even agrees he is such a man)? It would be much easier for him to change something he does in relation to you. You could suggest that he stop calling you names or looking lustfully at other women when you are together. These are actions that he can do differently.

If you decide that your daughter has a bad attitude, what is she supposed to do about that attitude (again, provided that she agrees)? Attitudes are hard to change. Instead, if she were willing, she could change things like slamming the door after you tell her something she doesn't like, or she could start coming home at curfew. Those are actions that she could theoretically change.

Vagueness also can be a problem when you and your partner have a different understanding or a different definition of the same word—and when you are in a conflict, usually you *do* have such differences. Moreover, in these tense moments each of you often interprets the other person's words in the most unhelpful, critical, hostile way. Saying, "You are afraid of intimacy," "You're just like your mother," or "You are oversensitive," does not communicate anything conducive to problem-solving. Saying, "We don't communicate," rarely leads to better communication.

But if you describe in "action" talk what the other person is doing, there is less tendency to blame (because you are not attacking inner qualities or motivations) and less likelihood of misunderstanding. This leads us to Solution Key 8.

Solution Key 8

USE ACTION TALK TO SOLVE RELATIONSHIP PROBLEMS

I'll break this key down into several elements that you can use in your relationships, whether with your spouse, with your family members, with friends, or with coworkers.

Action Talk, Method 1: Action Complaints

The first way to use action talk is to tell the person exactly what you are unhappy with—exactly what he or she did or does. I call this way of talking *action complaints.* Instead of focusing on the other person's qualities or intentions, or on any explanation you may have about why he or she did something, say only what action you were upset with.

Action Talk, Method 2: Action Requests

Action requests are the next step in resolving relationship problems. This time, instead of complaining about what the other person has done or is doing, you are going to say what you would like him or her to do in the future. Instead of saying to your partner, "I don't like how controlling you are," it works much better to say something like, "I would like to drive the car some of the time," or "I'd like you to wait until I'm done talking before you respond to the point I'm making." Instead of saying to your child, "You are such a slob! What do you think I am, your personal slave?," you could say, "I'd like you to put your dishes in the kitchen sink when you leave the living room." When you are called in for extra time at work, instead of saying, "This place runs in a crisis mode all the time, and I'm sick of it," you could try making a request like, "I'd like to have at least twenty-four hours notice when you are asking me to come in for extra time, so I can adjust my plans."

One couple who came for marriage counseling were on the verge of divorce. James was a recovering alcoholic who had stopped drinking about a year earlier. Sandy had expected him to change once he was sober. Now she had concluded that alcoholism had not been the problem; rather, James was cold and selfish as a person. He didn't care about anybody but himself. "Instead of drinking all the time," Sandy said with disgust, "now he works all the time or goes to AA meetings every night of the week. He never spends any time with me and our child." She had finally become so desperate that she had told him the night before this session that she was planning to seek a divorce. James agreed that he had been self-absorbed, both during his drinking years and since he'd been sober. But he contended that he could change. He vowed that if she would delay the divorce action, he would mend his ways. She agreed to give him a chance.

When they returned for another appointment two weeks later, however, they were both discouraged. He thought he had really gone out of his way to change his behavior for her and their family, but she didn't see any change. I asked James what he had done to show Sandy that he wasn't cold, selfish, and self-absorbed. "A lot," he told me, "but she didn't notice." "Give me one example," I suggested. "Well, yesterday, she came home from work with a bag of groceries in her arms. I put down the paper I was reading and met her at the front door, took the groceries from her, unpacked them, and put them away in the cupboards and refrigerator. I also cooked the vegetable for dinner last night."

I thought this effort deserved some credit, but Sandy was quick to correct me. "I could hire an assistant if I wanted help with the groceries and the cooking. I want a husband! I want someone who cares about me, who talks to me, who listens to me."

After some discussion, I asked Sandy to teach me and her husband what her husband could have done that would have looked like loving, caring behavior to her yesterday. She replied that all she really wanted was for James to ask her how her day was each night after work and to listen attentively to her for fifteen minutes. She said that, night after night, he would rant and rave for an hour or so about his day and his troubles, but would never ask her how her day had been. She said he had asked her once, several years before, how her day had been. She happened to have had a terrible day and had spent the next thirty minutes telling him about it. He never asked again, she said. James didn't think that he *never* asked about her day, but he agreed to listen to her talk about her day for fifteen minutes each weeknight (she gave him the weekends off) for the next two weeks. Sandy was skeptical that he would be able to do it, but he came through. That didn't resolve all of their marriage problems, of course, but it gave Sandy the sense that he could change, and so she stuck around to work out the rest of their problems.

Action requests usually have several elements that make them more likely to succeed. It is important not only to talk about a specific action, but to *let the other person know when or how often you would like the action to be performed.* Instead of saying, "I'd like you to take me out to dinner more often," you are more likely to get the result you want if you ask, "I'd like you to take me out to dinner at least three times a month."

It is also important sometimes to specify *who is to take what action* in a situation. In the above situation, your partner may agree to take you out to dinner three times per month, but who is going to call and make the reservations? Who will arrange a baby-sitter for the kids? If you are dating, who will pay for the meal? Who will decide on the restaurant?

A couple came to see me for marriage counseling. The wife's main complaint was that her husband "didn't respect her." He disagreed. He believed he respected her. Using the idea of action complaints and action requests, I asked her to cite a recent time when her husband had shown a lack of respect. The wife told about a party they had attended a few weeks before—while they were chatting with a group of people, he had snorted after she gave her opinion on a political issue. Obviously, she wanted him not to snort when she gave an opinion, but what else could he do, actively, to show respect in a similar situation in the future? (Here comes the action request.) She said that he could walk over and stand next to her after she made the comment, hold her hand, put his arm around her, and perhaps, introduce her to other people she didn't know at the party who had heard the remark. All this would indicate to her that he respected her, even if he disagreed with her opinion, because he would be letting others know that she was his wife.

Action Talk, Method 3: Action Praise

Of course, this wouldn't be a solution-oriented chapter if we didn't discuss the importance of attending to and speaking about what works or has worked in the relationship as a way to resolve problems. This is the third action talk method, called *action praise*: telling the other person what you appreciated about what he or she did in the past. Action praise involves describing current or past actions that you liked. For example, "I like it when you call me on my lunch break. It makes me feel loved to know that you are spontaneously thinking about me like that." The crucial element here is to be specific. That increases the likelihood that the other person will clearly understand what he or she is getting credit for and what to do more of in the future.

THE DIFFERENCE BETWEEN A RUT AND A GRAVE IS THE DIMENSIONS: CHANGING RELATIONSHIP PATTERNS

Years ago I read a book entitled *The Mirages of Marriage* by William J. Lederer and Don D. Jackson that captured the essence of a new way of thinking about relationships. The authors referred to a relationship pattern they called the "ten-foot pole." One person is telling the other (through actions or words), "I want more time and more commitment from you." The other is withdrawing, saying (again by actions or words), "I want more space; I feel pressured or pursued." Interestingly, if you ask either person, he or she will tell you that the problem exists inside the other. The one who is pursuing knows that the other one has a problem with commitment and intimacy. The one who is withdrawing thinks the other is insecure, perhaps codependent, and fears being alone. But if you look at their interactions objectively, you can see they are triggering each other's response. It is as if they have an invisible ten-foot pole between them. The more one pursues, the more the other is pushed away. The more one withdraws, the more the other is pulled to pursue. After a time, the pattern becomes repetitive.

This is the essence of the "systems" view of relationships. No one is completely independent. We are connected and responsive to our environment and to each other. The good news about this is that when we have relationship problems, no individual is solely at fault, and either person in the relationship can do something different to create a new "system" or pattern. In the ten-foot pole pattern, for example, if the person who is distancing can begin to move closer to the pursuer and stop withdrawing, the pursuer will probably stop pursuing so desperately. If you usually get loud during an argument, try keeping your voice soft one time and see what happens. Does your partner respond in a way that is different from usual?

My advice is this: When something is happening in your relationship that you don't like, instead of analyzing your partner, friend, business colleague, parent, etc., try doing something different. Break up your part of the pattern and find out if that changes the other person's response. If both of you are committed to making some changes, you can work on the patterns you will break together. If not, you can still change your part of the pattern and usually make a difference in the relationship pattern.

If you usually argue in the bedroom, go to the public library

The Solution-Oriented Relationship

1. *Acknowledge and validate* one another's feelings and points of view.
2. After acknowledgment and validation comes communication about *actions.* Tell each other which actions you experience as loving and intimate and which actions don't work for you.
3. Next, *learn to recognize and change problem patterns of actions.* If you find yourself doing the same thing over and over again, but it doesn't work, get the message! Do something different. If you used to do things that worked better, then do those things again. This may seem obvious, but when you are in a rut, sometimes you can't see the obvious.

and have the same discussion by writing it out on paper to one another and passing notes. If you usually fall asleep in front of the evening news, go bowling or dancing some night. Break out of your rut by doing something completely out of character for you. If you continue to do what you usually do, you'll probably continue to get the usual responses and results.

Relationship Rescue

NINE METHODS FOR RESOLVING RELATIONSHIP CRISES

Some time ago, I came across a flower essence called Rescue Remedy that is used in alternative medicine. When you have an emotional or health crisis, practitioners believe you can use this scent to calm down or heal. I thought it would be nice to have a similar rescue remedy for relationship crises and impasses. This section is designed to be your relationship Rescue Remedy to help you quickly break through impasses and resolve crises. Use any of these methods that make sense to you and that work.

---

1. Change Your Usual Conflict Patterns or Style

If you usually get loud during an argument, soften your voice. If you usually run away or withdraw, stay put. If you usually try to argue your point of view with a lawyer's precision and aggressiveness, just state your feelings about the matter and let it rest. If you usually interrupt to rebut what he is saying, just listen until he is done talking, then repeat what he has said back to him and ask whether you have understood his point or his feelings. If you usually point your finger during an argument, sit on your hands. Try changing the mode of expression you usually use to communicate. If you usually talk, switch to writing out what you have to say on a piece of paper. Or record your comments on a cassette and ask your partner to listen to it in another room.

Change the location or the timing of your usual conflict patterns or style. Instead of arguing in the living room, go to the front seat of the car or to a restaurant to argue. If you usually argue late at night, make an appointment for the next afternoon and have the argument then. Or limit the argument to ten minutes using the kitchen timer and then take a break for ten minutes, getting some physical distance from one another and remaining silent. Then argue another ten minutes, followed by another ten minutes of silence. Continue this pattern until the issue is resolved or until you both agree to stop.

---

2. Do a 180: Change Your Usual Pursuer-Distancer Pattern

This is a variation on method 1, but it is more specific. Most couples fall into a typical pattern of who pursues and who withdraws, both in the relationship in general and during conflicts. Figure out which part of the pattern you usually play out and change your style (from the person who withdraws to the person who stays or pursues or vice versa). Of course, both of you can make these changes or either one of you may do so.

---

3. Catch Your Partner Doing Something Right

Make note of and speak to your partner about everything in the recent past that you can think of to give him or her credit for. Speak about times when you felt cared about, helped, or understood by your partner and the specific things he or she did that led you to feel this way. Mention actions that you admired or were pleasantly surprised about. Catch your partner doing or almost doing something you want done differently, and praise him or her for it. Notice when your partner does something during an argument that seems more fair, more compassionate, or more friendly or that helps you to resolve things.

Hint: You can also catch yourself doing something right and silently give yourself credit. But note that being righteous—that is, making yourself right and your partner wrong—is not encouraged. Rather, notice when you are being flexible, compassionate, and understanding.

---

4. Unpack Vague, Blaming, and Loaded Words; Instead, Use Action Talk

Notice what words you are using that get a rise out of your partner and find a way to use less loaded or provocative words or phrases. For example, you might find that your partner reacts badly when you say things like, "You're being selfish," or "You're just like your father." The simplest way to defuse such phrases and words is to translate them into action talk. Instead of saying, "Well, when you were judging me, I got defensive," you could try saying, "When you pointed your finger at me and said I was immature, I got defensive."

---

5. Change Your Complaints into "Action Requests"

Probably the most crucial area for action talk is telling your partner what is bothering you about the relationship. Instead of indicting the other person for personality flaws or for having the wrong feelings, describe his or her behavior in action talk, and make action requests. This usually seems less blaming and is more likely to give a hint about what your partner might change to make things better. Instead of, "You are too sensitive," try, "I would like you to tell me when you are upset rather than going out without telling me." Instead of, "We never go out anymore because you don't like to do anything," try, "I would like to go out to the movies with you at least once every two weeks."

---

6. Make a Specific Plan for Change

Often we do better at making changes if we sit and plan a strategy of action, write it down, and check regularly on what we have written. This can be done with or without your partner. In making such a plan, it is important to include specific actions that you, your partner, or both of you are going to take, a time line for taking such actions or a commitment to how frequently you will take the actions, and a plan for how and when to check back on the plan to see if it's working or to make adjustments. For example, if you both agree that you would like to spend more time alone without the children, make a plan for which of you is going to arrange a baby-sitter, who is going to make reservations for the restaurant or call about the movie, and so on. Or if you decide that you would like to work on increasing your intimacy, make a plan for what activities you will do (such as reading aloud to one another or giving each other back rubs), how often you will do those activities, and some specific times and dates to check in with each other to make sure you have followed through with the planned actions—or to plan other actions if those didn't work.

---

7. Focus on How You (Not Your Partner) Can Change, and Take Responsibility for Making That Change

Even if your partner is the source of the problem, this method involves assuming responsibility yourself for making changes. This is based on the systems idea that people are responsive to changes around them. If you stop doing the tango and start doing the foxtrot, your partner will have a harder time doing the old tango steps. So figure out places in the usual course of things that go wrong but in which you have a moment of choice to do something different and new that isn't harmful or destructive.

---

8. Blow Your Partner's Stereotype of You

Sometimes the people we live with get a stereotyped impression of who we are, and we confirm that by always playing our typical roles. Figure out what your partner's stereotype of you is (you never do any work around the house, or you are always critical when your partner wants to watch football) and make a determined effort to shatter his or her expectations. Surprise yourself and your partner by doing something that would be entirely out of character for you. (But again, make sure it is not destructive or mean-spirited).

---

9. Compassionate Listening

Sometimes the simplest solution is to just stop and listen to what your partner is saying and imagine how he or she could be feeling that way or seeing things in that light. Don't try to defend yourself.

Don't try to correct your partner's perceptions. Don't try to talk your partner out of his or her feelings. Just put yourself in your partner's position and try to hear how he or she understands, interprets, and feels about the situation, and imagine how you would feel or act if your were seeing things that way. Express that understanding and say you know how difficult it must be for your partner, given his or her feelings about the situation.

When you are stuck in a relationship problem, things can seem hopeless. This section has given you some ideas and methods you can use to get yourself unstuck. Of course, if problems persist or you find yourself too discouraged to even consider these methods, it is wise to seek the help of a marriage or relationship counselor.

Relationship Refreshers

FOUR RELATIONSHIP STRENGTHENERS

Here are some suggestions that you can use when things aren't actually at a crisis to strengthen your relationships or to solve relationship problems.

1. If It Ain't Broke . . .

First, don't throw the baby out with the bathwater. If things are going well in some area, you don't have to change that area or doubt yourself or the relationship. Determine what is working and do more of that.

2. Stop Listening to Experts.

These days, you can find yourself doing something kind or compassionate for your partner and wonder if you are being "codepen-

Solution Key 8

USE ACTION TALK TO SOLVE RELATIONSHIP PROBLEMS

A simple way to solve relationship problems involves using action talk, i.e., words and phrases that describe rather than explain, analyze or blame. There are three ways to do action talk:

Method 1: **Action complaints**
Get specific and descriptive about what you don't like about what the other person has been doing or is doing. Stay away from blame and analysis.

Method 2: **Action requests**
Get specific and descriptive about what you would like the other person to start doing in the present and the future.

Method 3: **Action praise**
Let the other person know specifically what actions you have appreciated and would like him or her to continue to do in the future.

dent." Or you can read a magazine article and suddenly decide that your relationship doesn't really pass muster according to the article's guidelines. Reading suggestions for "Ten Ways to Jump-Start Your Man," may be just as likely to ground his battery as to turn him on. You are your own relationship expert. Trust your intuition and your common sense. Don't let outside experts (not just the ones in magazines or on television talk shows, but also your well intentioned friends, coworkers, or relatives) talk you out of something you like or into something that you know isn't right for you.

3. Do Something Different

It's been said that the only difference between a rut and a grave is the dimensions, and some couples have gotten into pretty deep ruts. Try changing anything you do in the relationship. (Keep it ethical and safe, of course.) If you are usually the one who is tight with money, encourage your partner to buy some extravagant present for himself or herself. If you usually don't notice chores that need to be done around the house, surprise your partner by initiating some chore. Break out of your usual ruts by doing something completely out of character for you. If you continue to do what you usually do, you'll most probably continue to get the usual responses and results.

4. Find a Different Way to Look at It

There's an old saying: Nothing is as dangerous as an idea when it is the only one you have. We are all prisoners of our limited point of view and we have a tendency to think our point of view is the only correct way of seeing things, especially when we are upset. So, when you are stuck or unhappy, find another way of looking at the situation. Think of it from another angle. For example, how would you be thinking of this situation if the other person were your child or your best friend rather than your spouse or partner?

CHAPTER 10

YOU MEAN YOU CAN TALK DURING THIS?

Solution-Oriented Sexuality

Sex is one of the nine reasons for incarnation. . . .
The other eight are unimportant.

—Henry Miller

Few areas are as fraught with difficulty as sexuality. Most people are embarrassed to talk about the subject openly. Some suffer from fears that they are not "normal" or that they are not performing up to standard. Others suffer from shame that springs from their upbringing, either from messages they got regarding the shamefulness of sex or from the aftereffects of being sexually abused. In this chapter I will try to address this subject in a straightforward way and provide a solution-oriented sensibility as a way to approach sexuality and to solve sexual problems.

Steps in Solution-Oriented Sexuality

Here, succinctly, are the main steps in solution-oriented sexuality:

- Step 1: Avoid analyzing, labeling, or judging yourself or others in a negative way for what you or they desire or feel sexually. Just acknowledge your and their sexual fantasies, desires, wants, sensations, and so on. Outside experts (psychologists, psychiatrists, friends, family members, religious leaders, self-help books, popular magazines, and television shows) have no right to define for consenting adults what is right for them sexually. When it comes to the "inside" part of sexuality, there is no absolute "right" or "wrong."

  Shows like HBO's *Real Sex*, studies like the Kinsey Report on Human Sexuality, the proliferation of alternative sexuality sites on the Internet, the availability of adult videos, and more and more open discussions in the media about sexual issues have shown that this area has been hidden and mystified for years. Our private behavior never measured up to our puritanical standards or to the homogeneity we thought was prevalent in our society regarding sexual behavior and preferences. The range of "normal" is wider than we have been led to believe.
- Step 2: When it comes to action, though, some things work and some don't. So, first, speak up for what you want, but don't demand it or force it on someone else. Second, speak clearly, using action talk to communicate to your partner what you haven't liked or don't like

about what he or she has done sexually with you (sexual action complaints); about what you would like to do in the future (sexual action requests); and what you have liked about what he or she has done sexually in the past (sexual action praise).

- Step 3: Recall and recreate what has worked sexually for you and the other person in the past and use that to enhance your current sexual relationship or to solve sexual problems you are currently facing.
- Step 4: Use the information gathered in steps 2 and 3 to negotiate a mutually agreeable and pleasurable sex life. Find areas of agreement and ways to compromise on areas of disagreement, if possible. Remember that you are negotiating in the realm of actions, not desires or the inner experience of sexuality. Do not invalidate or try to change the other person's feelings or wishes. Instead, focus on changes in actions. If you are stuck, try changing relationship patterns in general and sexual patterns specifically. Go to a hotel for the weekend or dress up in some sexy clothes. Or read an erotic book aloud to each other.

Principles of Solution-Oriented Sexuality

When You're Hot, You're Hot; and When You're Not, You're Not

The first thing to say about sexuality is what the comedian Flip Wilson said years ago: *When you're hot, you're hot; and when you're not, you're not!* Don't try to force yourself to feel sexual excitement when you are not feeling it. Sometimes when men lose their erections, they become self-conscious and try to force what had been a natural process of sexual excitement. Of course, this usually has exactly the opposite effect. The same goes for women with regard to getting lubricated and sexually excited. Sometimes, lack of sexual excitement may be just temporary or due to a situation. For example, you may be tired or distracted by some problem at work, and much as you try to forget it, it interferes with your letting go enough to get into the sexual experience. In that case, just accepting this lack of excitement can help you let it go and not turn it into a problem. The next time, things will probably work just fine. Or the lack of sexual excitement may be due to more long-term factors, such as a medical condition or medications that interfere with arousal or response. (It's always best to check with a physician in such cases.) Or it may be an indication of boredom or problems in your sexual relationship or in your relationship in general. Regardless of the reason for the lack of arousal, the suggestion remains the same. Don't try to force yourself to become aroused.

Doing Sex: Solution-Oriented Sexuality

On the other hand, sometimes there are things you can deliberately do to create arousal. We used to believe that we had to have a feeling before we took action, but modern approaches to therapy and psychology have shown that sometimes feelings can be created or evoked by action. If you aren't feeling sexual, sometimes doing sexual things can evoke a sexual response. Sometimes it's late at night, you've had a long day, and both you and your partner are tired. You turn to each other, knowing that it has been too long since you have had sex. "Do you want to?" one of you asks. "I'm tired but I'm up for it if you are," the other replies. If you then begin to do sexual things with each other, you usually begin to feel more aroused and less tired.

If you are having sexual problems, you can also search for actions and ideas that have worked in the past and do them deliberately.

A young woman consulted me. "I'm not sure I really need counseling," she said. "My fiancé says I've got a problem and he thinks that if I don't get it taken care of before we get married, I'll be unhappy in the marriage." "What kind of problem is it?" I asked. She was very embarrassed, but finally, after several minutes of uncomfortable silence, she blurted out, "It's a sexual problem." I asked, "What kind of sexual problem?" "I don't have orgasms when we have sex," she said. "My fiancé is afraid that if I never have orgasms, I'll become dissatisfied with the marriage or have an affair sometime." "Is this your first sexual relationship?" I asked. She said, "No, he's my third serious relationship. I went with a guy in high school for several years. He was the first guy I had sex with. Then, after we broke up, I went with another guy for about six months. We had sex too, but I never had an orgasm with him." "Wait a minute," I said; "do you mean you had orgasms with your first boyfriend?" "Yes, a few times," she replied. "Well," I said, "in thinking back on that relationship, was there anything that you think helped you have orgasms during sex with that boyfriend? Did you trust him more than you do your fiancé, or did you talk more openly about what you wanted, or were you using birth control and were therefore more relaxed, or did you have manual stimulation or oral stimulation or a different sexual position that helped?" "Well, now that I think about it, it was usually when we had oral sex," she replied. "When he did oral sex to you, you had orgasms more often?" "Yes." "Did you ever have an orgasm with your fiancé? And if so, what helped?" "Once I did. When he did oral sex with me." "He's done oral sex other times, but you haven't had an orgasm?" "No, he's only done it the one time." "And you were able to have an orgasm. Why do you think he's never done it again? Are you or he uncomfortable with it?" "No, I don't think so. He's just never done it again." "Have you ever told him that oral sex helps you have an orgasm?" "No. Do you think I should?" "Yes," I said dryly, "I think that might be a good idea." "Great," she said, standing up quickly, "I'll give it a try!" She returned two weeks later, triumphant. "It worked!" "Great!" I said. But I wasn't too surprised. It turned out that she knew very well how to have orgasms. She just didn't realize she knew. She had a ready solution to what she and her fiancé saw as a difficult problem.

The point I'm making here is that sex is a combination of feelings, ideas, and actions. As I discussed in the earlier chapters of the book, you can change your actions, your stories (points of view and beliefs), and your attention to change your sexual life and solve sexual problems. I'll tell you another story to illustrate this.

I saw a couple who said that passion had gone out of their thirty-year relationship. They reported that during the early years of the relationship, they had had quite a wonderful and varied sexual relationship but that it had dissipated over the years, to the point where it had been some years since they had any sexual contact at all. The wife attributed the loss of intimacy to the fact that her husband had some years ago gone out and bought her a "dream vacation," a backpacking trip through Nepal, as a surprise. The wife was surprised indeed and told him that the vacation he had arranged was not the kind she wanted to take. The husband canceled the reservations. The wife felt he was resentful, and that this had brought about a subtle estrangement, which they had never discussed because the incident had been so painful for them both. She assumed that this was the reason they had not had sex much since that time. The husband, hearing his wife's explanation, said that in fact it wasn't why he hadn't been initiating sex. When asked why, he sheepishly admitted that the main reason was that she had gained a lot of weight. He hadn't wanted to hurt her feelings by mentioning it and also was keenly aware of the fact that he had gained quite a bit of weight as well, so it wasn't really fair to criticize her. Nevertheless, this had diminished his sexual interest. Both of them had recently started active exercise and diet programs to begin losing weight. It would take some time, however, for the effects of these programs to be seen. I therefore focused the couple on immediate actions they could take to improve their sexual intimacy. I asked them to describe what they used to do when they had had a "hot" (their word) sexual relationship. They described themselves as sexual adventurers who liked to vary their lovemaking locations and practices. I suggested that they try to act as they did when they had been passionate lovers. When the couple returned for their next session, they reported that they had gone home the evening following the session, had immediately had sex, and had had lots of "hot" sex since. They were pleasantly surprised to find that actions had created feelings.

Why Sex Is Like Back-scratching: Action Talk in Sex

Sex is like back-scratching because you have to let the other person know what you want and what feels good to you. When you ask a person to scratch your back, you give some coaching, "No, down a little and to the left, right there, yes, a little harder. Yes, that's it, thanks." You don't expect the other person to know, without your saying, what works and what doesn't. But in our sexual lives, we expect the other person to know what works without being told or coached.

I know about this problem, since I was very shy when I was young, and I had been raised in a religion that gave messages that sex was not a thing to be talked about. That was two strikes against my ever communicating with my partner about what I or she wanted, what felt good or felt bad.

The first sexual encounters I had, then, were mysterious and a bit frightening to me. Was I doing it correctly? Was my partner enjoying the experience? Did she have an orgasm? Did she want me to do something different? Did she want to continue or have sex again? Because I had little experience, I had read up on the subject, but the reality was so different from the descriptions in the books that my academic preparation didn't really help much. There was no way I was going to ask these questions, because I was too shy and too afraid of looking inexperienced. Unfortunately, my partners followed my lead and we never spoke about what was working and what was not. We never told each other new things we'd like to try.

After several relationships, I met a woman who was quite uninhibited and open about sex. When we first started to have a sexual relationship, she began telling me things she would like me to do: "Ooh, lick my nipple, a little harder, ooh, yes, that's good." And "Rub my clitoris between your fingers. No, that's too hard. Yes, that's about right." I was shocked. I thought, *You mean I can talk during this?* That was nothing compared with what came next. She began to ask *me* what I wanted *her* to do. And she began to try different sexual stimulations with me and ask me whether I liked them or not. *You mean I have to talk during this?* After I got over my initial discomfort, I found that I really preferred this way of sexual interaction. It reminded me of back-scratching. Why shouldn't we let our partners know what feels good and what doesn't? This kind of specific communication can eliminate an untold amount of anxiety and shame in your sexual life.

You may have noticed that this harks back to our discussion in Chapter 9 about using action language: action complaints, action requests, and action praise. But this time, I am suggesting that you use these methods specifically in relation to sex.

One couple I worked with found that they were too inhibited to actually talk to each other about their sexual likes and dislikes. So I suggested that they first try writing each other letters after each sexual encounter, saying what had worked and what they had appreciated, as well as what they would like to have happen differently in future sexual encounters.

In working with one couple who had difficulty communicating about their sex life, I got up and wrote two lists on the blackboard in my office. "Okay," I said, "pick one from each list and connect them. Choose one from column A and one from column B." They were able to use this list to begin the process of communicating and exploring preferences for their sexual life together. Here's the list. You might want to use it (or add to it) with a partner to open up your sex life.

Mix-and-Match Sexual Menu

A	B
Fingers	Mouth
Tongue	Clitoris
Mouth	Penis
Penis	Vagina
Vagina	Breast
Hand	Nipples
	Anus
	Skin

Negotiate Differences

Often, two people have different sexual desires or preferences. How do we deal with those differences in the solution-oriented approach? First, make sure you are negotiating about things you will do together. As we've noted, trying to change someone's inner life—his or her sexual desires and preferences—is out of bounds in this approach. Also, do not label or analyze others in a negative way, creating stories about what is wrong with them (or yourself, for that matter).

Instead, it's most effective to focus the negotiations on making changes in the realm of actions, that is, what you will do with each other sexually or what you will do individually.

I counseled a couple who were having conflicts about the frequency of sex. He thought she was unreasonable because she wanted to have sex only once a week or so. He wanted to have sex at least four or five times per week—every day if possible. She thought he was a sex fiend and needed to deal with his "sexual addiction." Clearly, this mutual invalidation was not helping them solve their sexual differences. After I got them to stop invalidating, blaming, and shaming each other, we began the negotiations. The first break we got was that she had assumed that each time he wanted to have sex, he was asking for intercourse. We discovered that sometimes he would be just as happy if she rubbed his thighs while he masturbated, which she was perfectly happy to do. Also—and this was something he was very ashamed of—he had been secretly cruising the Internet late at night after she went to bed, searching for pornography. He felt that by hiding this from her, he was betraying her. She didn't judge him harshly for this, although she preferred that he not keep such shameful secrets from her. They decided that once a month they would watch an adult video together, and he agreed to stop secretly and compulsively cruising the Internet. He was surprised when it turned out that she was very turned on by some of the pornography. This challenged his idea that she wasn't as sexual as he was and that therefore they could never have a mutually satisfying sexual life.

Ask for What You Want, but Don't Demand It

While it is important to ask for what you want and to speak up about what you like, be careful not to force something on your partner that is not right for him or her. People don't usually respond well in sexual situations when they are feeling uncomfortable or are forced to participate in something they don't like. So make sure you are not coercing or forcing your partner. At the same time, sometimes people don't speak up about what they desire or would like to try because they are afraid their partner wouldn't like it or would disapprove. You can at least bring the subject up to your partner and let him or her know there is no demand, but there is an interest in trying some sexual behavior.

Get Creative

Get out of ruts. Try new positions, locations, talk, clothes, toys, and so on. If it feels right, read each other fantasies you have found in books or magazines or written out on your own.

Schedule Time

Don't always leave sex until late at night or assume it will happen spontaneously. You may have to schedule time out of your busy work, social, or family life for sexual encounters. Again, the key here is to take the pressure off. You are scheduling time to allow sexual interactions, but if the timing or the situation isn't right, just use that time to reconnect in any way you can. You might just give each other back rubs, or talk, or snuggle. If sex happens, great! If not, relax and enjoy this special time together.

Fantasies and Desires Don't Necessarily Equal Identity or Lead to Behavior

Just because you fantasize about things, it doesn't necessarily indicate that you want to act those things out or have them happen in the real world. You may fantasize about being raped or having sex with someone of the same sex, but you may never want to experience that in reality.

This can also hold true for your sexual identity. Many people are attracted to people of the same sex but don't define themselves as homosexual. Likewise, sometimes people who are homosexual are attracted to people of the opposite sex but still think of themselves as gay or lesbian. Your sexual identity is partly a matter of what makes you feel comfortable and what attracts you, but it is mainly a function of how you choose to define yourself. You may not have much choice about what or who turns you on, but your identity is much more a matter of choice and preference. Some people live their whole lives being primarily attracted to one sex, yet define themselves in a very different way. Call it denial or whatever you will, but sexual identity is a political act and each person must sort out his or her own politics.

The point is that you can let yourself feel, fantasize, or think anything you desire sexually. This need not determine your choices in life or define you.

In Search of the Big O

Don't get so hung up on the goal that you ignore or rush the process. Trying too hard to have an orgasm can prevent you from having one or from fully enjoying it when it arrives. On the other hand, if you never or rarely have orgasms, you can make adjustments so that this becomes a more regular part of your sexual experience. Use the other suggestions I have given above to enhance the likelihood of experiencing orgasms.

What about premature ejaculation? Slow down; stop moving; pay attention to when his orgasm is approaching. Many men feel they have to perform or keep moving to give their partners pleasure. Delaying ejaculation is a skill that can be learned. Work together to help him learn to slow down and enjoy the process.

What about having simultaneous orgasms? It is possible, again with good communication and with taking the pressure off. Some couples have this experience quite regularly and others have such different timing that they are unlikely to coordinate their orgasms.

Summary of Solution-Oriented Sexuality

1. When you're hot, you're hot; and when you're not, you're not

Just acknowledge and accept your sexual feelings (or lack of feelings). Trying to force yourself or others to feel something you or they don't will usually have the opposite of the intended effect. It will make you or them even less excited. Relax and let the feelings flow. If there is a persistent lack of arousal, there may be medical issues or other relationship or personal issues to be resolved.

2. Doing sex: solution-oriented sexuality

Find times in the past when things have worked well sexually, and deliberately do what you can to evoke or re-create those times. If you can't recall such times or if trying these things doesn't help, try changing anything (thoughts, what you are attending to, actions, interactions, settings, etc.) to change things sexually.

3. Why sex is like back-scratching: action talk in sex

Use action talk to describe explicitly what you don't like about what your partner is doing sexually, what you would like him or her to do in the future, and what you have liked about what he or she has done in the past.

4. Negotiate differences

Do not focus on changing your partner's insides (his or her desires or sexual preferences), but instead focus on finding mutually agreeable actions that would work for both of you.

5. Ask for what you want, but don't demand it

Trying to force someone to do something sexually is usually a big turnoff. Don't shame others for not desiring something you think they should want or enjoy—and don't shame yourself for not desiring something that someone else wants.

6. Get creative

Sex can get repetitious and routine. To reawaken interest and creativity, try varying anything that you usually do sexually.

7. Schedule time

In today's busy world, sometimes it is necessary to schedule time to have sex. Remember not to force it, but you can start to do some sexual things during this scheduled time and find out if you get into it. If you don't, just enjoy the time in another way.

8. Fantasies and desires don't necessarily equal identity or lead to behavior

Just because you fantasize something, it doesn't necessarily mean that you really want it to happen in the real world. Let yourself have free rein in the realm of fantasy. Then decide whether or not you want to talk about your fantasies or act them out.

Also, desiring something doesn't entirely define you as a person. You might have a fantasy about having sex with someone of the same gender, but that doesn't make you homosexual any more than fantasizing about having sex with a person of the opposite gender disqualifies a gay person from being gay.

9. In search of the big O

Don't get hung up on having an orgasm in every sexual encounter. Relax and enjoy the process. On the other hand, if you are never having orgasms or if one person in a couple is not having orgasms, there are things you can do to ensure that they happen more regularly and equitably.

CHAPTER 11

EXORCISING THE GHOSTS OF THE PAST

Using Rituals to Resolve Unfinished Business and to Prevent Problems

We don't need to learn how to let things go; we just need to learn to recognize when they've already gone.

—Suzuki Roshi

If, after using the solution-oriented methods in the previous chapters, you still have some unfinished business from the past, this chapter will give you a solution-oriented method to help you quickly resolve past traumas. The process involves the use of rituals.

We use two types of rituals in solution-oriented therapy. The first is the type that you typically do only once to help you move on from trauma. I call these *resolution rituals*. The second is a ritual that you do repeatedly and develop into a habit. This type of ritual is used both to prevent problems and to reestablish a sense of stability after a crisis or a change in your life. I call this type the *stability and connective ritual.*

Solution Key 9

PERFORM A RESOLUTION RITUAL TO RESOLVE UNFINISHED ISSUES FROM THE PAST

Rituals have been used by almost all cultures to help people make transitions and move on to different phases of life. Most religions use rituals for the same purpose. In the Jewish religion, a family sits shiva after the death of one of its members, going through ritual actions for prescribed periods. In the first week, the mirrors in the house are covered, family members wear black clothing, which is ripped, and they do not leave the home. There are other rituals for the next months. Then at the end of a year, prayers are said for the dead and a stone is left on the grave. In the Catholic religion, last rights (called extreme unction) are given to the dying person.

The main feature of these rituals is that they are special, time-limited actions that help people move on by giving them something to *do*. Instead of analyzing and dwelling on the past when you are stuck, then, you can use resolution rituals to move the unfinished business from bouncing around in your insides into the realm of action, where you can do something to resolve it.

Barb didn't really like her life. She was single, lonely, and unhappy in her job. She had health problems and was overweight. She had been sexually abused as a child, and she had never felt that she was really lovable. One day, at a supermarket, a man approached her and started a conversation. He asked her how to cook squash. She politely answered his query and moved on. The man casually followed her through the store. At first she was a bit annoyed and scared, but he was so charming that after a while, she spoke to him. Near the end of the shopping trip, Tom formally introduced himself and asked Barb to go out with him. Flattered, she agreed—still not sure of him, but intrigued and excited. Perhaps her life would take a turn for the better, she thought.

The next few months were blissful. Tom turned out to be quite romantic, bringing her flowers, calling daily, and writing her love poems. He was a successful businessman who earned $100,000 per year, he told her. They ended up falling in love and soon were having sex.

Then a few troubling signs began to surface. Tom refused to give Barb his home phone number or his address. He told her that he liked his privacy, and that if she needed to call, she could call him on his cellular phone, which he kept in his truck. He started telling her his fantasies about having sex with her and another woman. On occasion, he lied about little things. Still, aside from these minor complaints, the relationship was going well. Barb was happy for the first time in her life. Friends and coworkers told her that she was blossoming. She began to talk to Tom about getting married, and he seemed eager at the prospect.

One day, in a casual conversation, Barb happened to mention Tom's name to a neighbor, who asked if Tom's wife still worked at the telemarketing firm. Barb was stunned and thought the neighbor must have confused Tom with someone else. But when she investigated, she found out that Tom was indeed married and had a teenage son. When she confronted Tom with her discoveries, he became enraged at her "snooping." Later, he came to her house, confronted her, and, when she stood her ground, raped her. She never saw him again.

When Barb sought therapy, she was still upset and felt "unfinished" about the situation she had gotten herself into with Tom. She avoided people and was fearful of any man who showed an interest in her. She felt dirty, she said, especially her hair. Tom had admired her red hair and had once given her a very sensual shampoo. In discussing the situation, a song from the musical *South Pacific* came to mind: "I'm Gonna Wash that Man Right Outta My

Hair." With that start, Barb designed a ceremony in which she wrote Tom and her cousin (who had abused her in childhood) letters that expressed all her feelings of being deceived, violated, and abandoned. She then burned the letters, and washed her hair over and over again, listening to the song, until she felt she *had* washed Tom and her cousin right out of her life.

In order to do a resolution ritual, you need to find a symbol, that is, some physical object that relates to your trauma, problem, or unfinished business. It might be a picture of a person related to the trauma or a photo of you around the time that the trauma happened. It could be an object that is related to the trauma, such as a broken piece from a car in which you were riding that was involved in an accident. Next, design and carry out some activity that will symbolize moving on or leaving the old unfinished situation behind. It could be throwing the object into a lake or the ocean. It might involve burning it, burying it, or leaving it on someone's grave.

A man had an affair with his next-door neighbor. His wife discovered the affair one day when she found a key chain with the lover's name on it in the back corner of their closet. She confronted him and he confessed. The couple separated but then decided to try to work things out. After some months of counseling and lots of crying, yelling, and talking, they moved back together. But even though everything had been said, the wife still felt haunted by the affair. She couldn't seem to let go of her anger. A resolution ritual was designed that involved finding a key chain with the lover's name on it. That was the symbol.

The wife was to take the key chain and find a physical way to express her anger on the object—as opposed to expressing it physically on her husband or the neighbor, which she felt like doing! First she took it out to the back porch and beat on it with a hammer, but that didn't feel satisfying enough. After thinking for some time, she decided on the perfect ritual. She took the key chain and threw

SYMBOLS

Symbols are concrete objects that represent a person, place, inner experience, or situation and can be used to embody unresolved areas in your life or your relationships.

You may already have symbols of your unresolved areas (a photo, a key chain, a shirt) or you may need to create them by writing, drawing, sculpturing, sewing, or gathering or collecting items from nature.

it onto the street. Then she began to drive back and forth over it. That ritual finally resolved enough of the anger that she wasn't plagued with memories of the affair intruding so much on her daily life or her relationship with her husband.

You may do your resolution ritual alone or with someone else. Really think through where, with whom, and when would be the right time, place, and circumstances for the ritual. It might be on an anniversary or on some other significant date. It may be in some significant place.

Although Carrie had a loving relationship with a man she had been involved with for the past six months, she was depressed. She found herself brooding over her ex-husband and their marriage, which had ended in divorce several years ago. Her ex-husband had been physically brutal to her and the children, had often been drunk, and had frequently been unfaithful. Once, when he was angry, he had even tried to run over her and the children with the car.

I suggested that she draw a picture representing her marriage. She protested that she wasn't much of an artist, but I told her that her artwork would not be hanging in an art museum. It was to help her get free of her past. She drew a spiral that had more and more negative events on it, as though the relationship had been a whirlpool that had sucked her and her children into its treacherous vortex. When she returned for the next session, I told her to burn it. She decided to involve her current boyfriend in the ritual.

When she returned for the next session, she told me she was upset with me. I was perplexed. "Why?" I asked. She said, "If I had known that you were going to ask me to burn it, I would have made it huge so that I could have had the satisfaction of watching it burn for a very long time! It burned too quickly." I asked her if she needed to draw a larger picture and do the ritual again, but she said that the brooding had now stopped, so it wouldn't be necessary.

Make sure you are really ready, emotionally and psychologically, for the resolution ritual. The point here is not to force the matter, but to have something you can do to resolve things when you are ready to move on but haven't been able to let go despite your best efforts.

When I was in college, I had a girlfriend who had been raised in a difficult household. Her parents' marriage was quite stormy, and the kids had been routinely caught in the middle of the conflict, with each parent vying for their loyalty. When my girlfriend left for college, she thought she would escape being involved in the conflicts, but now and then she would receive letters from her mother that hooked her right back in: tirades about how terrible her father was and how my girlfriend always took his side. My girlfriend would get terribly upset reading these letters, so she finally asked me to screen each letter and warn her when it was a bad one. I agreed. She wouldn't read the bad ones, but I told her there was some good stuff even in the bad letters, so we decided that I would cut out the bad parts and give her the rest of the letter. Since I didn't feel right about throwing away the bad parts of the letters, I began to store them (face down, so she wouldn't accidentally read them) in a tea basket on my kitchen table. After a while, I started to feel creepy having all those hostile words hanging around my kitchen, so I suggested that my girlfriend take them home with her. "No way," she said. "I'm not having those negative vibes around my house, either!" After some discussion, we decided that she would address an envelope to her mother and we would put all these snippets in the envelope with a note from my girlfriend that said, "Dear Mom, Thanks for all the letters. I didn't want these parts. Love, your daughter." After that, she never received another nasty letter from her mother.

Resolution rituals can be used as part of the healing process in situations of grief and loss. But remember from Chapter 4 that it is important to acknowledge and not invalidate your own or others' feelings. Resolution rituals are not a way to escape the painful but normal grief process; these rituals are a way to help you move on when you are stuck, but ready to put the past behind you.

A couple had lost their young child to leukemia. Carolyn was a sweet child, and it had been terrible to watch helplessly as she went through the torture of the cancer treatments that ultimately had not saved her life. The hospital had become the couple's second home during the last months of Carolyn's life, and the medical personnel on the pediatric oncology unit their second family. After Carolyn died, the couple felt more than one void in their lives. Not only had they lost Carolyn; they had also lost their second family, since they no longer spent time at the hospital. As the anniversary of Carolyn's death approached, the couple began to worry that they would begin the painful grief process all over again, after the wounds had started to heal. We devised a ritual that involved planting a fruit tree in their backyard (Carolyn had loved eating fruit) and making plans to take a picture of the tree to the hospital staff on the anniversary. Thereafter, every year on the anniversary of Carolyn's death, they brought a picture—and some fruit from the tree—to the medical personnel at the hospital who had known Carolyn.

Solution Key 9

PERFORM A RESOLUTION RITUAL TO RESOLVE UNFINISHED ISSUES FROM THE PAST

Here is a step-by-step guide to creating a resolution ritual to complete unfinished business or resolve past traumas:

- Clarify what the purpose of the ritual is and what is still unfinished for you.
- Prepare for the ritual by deciding what symbols you will use, when you will perform the ritual, who else will be included, what you will wear, where you will perform the ritual, and what you need to do to get ready, emotionally and psychologically.
- Perform the ritual.
- If it is appropriate, arrange for friends, significant others, or family members to attend a celebration of the completion of the ritual and your determination to move on.

Solution Key 10

DEVELOP STABILITY AND CONNECTIVE RITUALS TO PREVENT PROBLEMS AND CREATE CONNECTIONS

There is a second way to use rituals to solve or, better yet, to prevent problems. That is to develop regular rituals or habits that help create stability and connect you to your life or to others in your life.

I was counseling a couple who had been married for thirty-five years. They came to me on the verge of a divorce. The wife complained that they had never had an intimate relationship. The husband, an engineer, had never been expressive about his feelings. The most he would do was criticize or be irritable. He might say what he thought, but he rarely told his wife how he felt. "The only feeling I know that he has is horniness," she said, "because he always wants to have sex." I told them it sounded as if the territory between his neck and his penis was a vast unknown land, and if they were to stay together, they would have to discover what was there. They agreed to try, but the problem was that much of the time, the man had no idea what he was feeling. "I'm usually the last one to know how I'm feeling," he joked. "She can usually tell me what I am feeling before I know it." After some discussion, I began to agree with him. He didn't seem to recognize any inner feelings.

I told the couple that to create intimacy we would have to start with some "baby steps" (with apologies to the movie *What About Bob?* for those of you who recognize that phrase from it). The husband was to find a book that both partners would like to read, and then initiate reading for fifteen minutes to half an hour each night. After the reading, he should initiate a discussion of their reactions to the book. He followed through with this connective ritual, and the couple began to feel the intimacy that had been missing from their marriage for so many years.

A friend of mine told me a charming story about developing a connective ritual. When he was first dating the woman who would later become his wife, Tim cooked dinner for her regularly at his house. After dinner, they would do the dishes together; he would wash and she would dry. They both enjoyed the after-dinner ritual of cleaning up and had some of their best conversations during that time. After several dates, his girlfriend noticed that Tim's kitchen had a dishwasher. She assumed it was broken and teased him about being a procrastinator for not getting it fixed. He defended himself by telling her that the dishwasher wasn't broken. "Why did we wash all those dishes by hand, then?" she asked in amazement. "The first night," Tim explained, "there were so few dishes that I thought it would be a waste to use the dishwasher. Then I realized that I enjoyed doing the dishes with you so much that I didn't tell you about the dishwasher for fear that you wouldn't want to do it anymore and we would be robbed of that special time." Washing dishes by hand became a regular ritual that connected this couple, and they use it to this day.

A stability and connective ritual, then, is anything you do repeatedly on your own or with someone else that connects you to yourself or the other in a positive way. It might be going for a walk every night, or writing in your journal before you go to sleep. It might be going out to a movie together every Saturday. It might be reading the Bible as a family one night a week after dinner.

Steve Wolin, the psychiatrist I mentioned earlier, conducted research on alcoholic families who unexpectedly didn't produce children as troubled as the children of other dysfunctional alcoholic families. The kids from the families in the study didn't grow up to be alcoholics or drug addicts and didn't even develop the classic problems of "adult children of alcoholics." Wolin found that one of the crucial factors protecting these kids was that their families had stability and connective rituals, which were kept intact despite the families' serious problems. These families celebrated birthdays and holidays, went regularly to church services together, had read or told bedtime stories every evening, or had meals together.

When I was growing up, one thing you could count on in my family of eight kids was that at dinnertime, at 6 P.M., everyone would be at the dinner table. You had to have an extraordinary excuse not to be there. Dinner was when we connected as a family. In the midst of the chaos of piano lessons, sports events, school activities, and so on, we could always count on this special time together every day.

We also had regular weekly rituals. We were Catholic, so we all

Solution Key 10

DEVELOP STABILITY AND CONNECTIVE RITUALS TO PREVENT PROBLEMS AND CREATE CONNECTIONS

- Stability and connective rituals are regularly repeated activities done alone or in groups that help create stability or a sense of connection with oneself or others.
- Stability and connective rituals can enhance intimacy and connections between people and can help people withstand stress and trauma.

dressed up and went to ten o'clock mass every Sunday. When our church started holding services on Saturday nights as an alternative to Sunday services, it disrupted my family's ritual, since some of us didn't like to get up early and opted out of the Sunday mass in favor of Saturday night. But for most of my developing years, this was another ritual I could count on in my family and in my life.

We had other rituals as well. On birthdays (which seemed to come every few weeks or so in that large a family), the birthday person would have to don a paper crown and be sung the birthday song. (Always twice! "Once more with gusto!" my father would bellow after the first rendition.) Then came the making of a silent wish, followed by trying to blow out all the candles in one breath (except when my brother substituted the trick candles that couldn't be blown out).

Christmas and Thanksgiving had their own traditions that made them rituals that we could count on every year.

Years later, Wolin's research showed that such stability and connective rituals have healthy effects on children, providing them with a sense of protection from harm even when they are in difficult, traumatic circumstances.

Exercise: Remembering and Reinstating Regular Habits

Think about any regular activity you have engaged in, either alone or with a family member. It could be going out for a movie once a week, reading books (out loud to others or on your own), walking, running or doing some other exercise, giving your partner a nightly foot rub, and so on. Given the current circumstances of your life, what regular ritual could you reasonably commit to doing for the next month? Make the commitment by writing it down or talking to others about it. After the month is up, check with yourself or the other person and decide if the ritual is right for you. If not, make whatever adjustment you need to make it work, or find another one. Perhaps you commited to doing it nightly when three times per week would be more realistic. Perhaps the activity used to work but now no longer fits into your life.

CHAPTER 12

IF YOU FALL ON YOUR FACE, AT LEAST YOU'RE HEADING IN THE RIGHT DIRECTION

Solution-Oriented Living

> Such is life, falling over seven times and getting up eight.
>
> —Roland Barthes, *A Lover's Discourse*

In this book, I have tried to introduce you to a way of thinking and living that I believe can make a profound difference in your life. Let me summarize the principles of solution-oriented living here.

Principles of Solution-Oriented Living

1. It's important to acknowledge how you are feeling and what you have been through, but the past and your feelings do not automatically determine what you do now or in the future. They

do not entirely define you, but it is crucial that you acknowledge them.

2. It is better to pay attention to what works than to spend a lot of time and energy analyzing why things don't work or what is wrong with you or with someone else.
3. The first place to look for what works is to recall what worked in the past in circumstances similar to what you are facing now.
4. Next, examine what you keep doing over and over again in any of the following areas:
    - Actions
    - Interactions you have with others
    - What you are paying attention to
    - What you are thinking or telling yourself (your stories about life, your problem, other people, or yourself)

   If what you are doing is not working, try doing something different. Change your patterns and find out if the problem changes.
5. Focus on the future that you would like to have instead of the past or present that you don't like. Talk as if that future is possible and likely. Be specific about where you would like to be, and what you would be doing when you get there. Acknowledge and deal with barriers, real or imagined, that prevent you from getting to that future. Take action steps to begin to move toward and create that future.
6. You can use spirituality, which offers ways of rising above both your everyday life and your limited beliefs and selfish concerns, to transcend and resolve problems.
7. In relationships, avoid the traps represented by blame, labeling, and analysis. Be specific regarding what you don't like about what others have done or are doing. Then let them know what you would like them to do instead. Give them credit for the

things that they have done that you have appreciated and would like them to continue doing or do more of in the future. Change patterns if problems keep repeating. One person can change a two-person relationship by changing his or her part of the interpersonal pattern.

8. In the realm of sexuality, it is crucial to realize that what you feel and desire is not bad, wrong, or abnormal. Accept your own and others' desires and preferences. Communicate with your partner specifically and clearly about what you would like, what is working, and what is not working about your sexual interactions (again, without blaming or labeling).
9. If, after trying these strategies, you find that you are still stuck or still feel unfinished about some issue in the past, you can use a resolution ritual to help you move on. Find a symbolic object that represents the unfinished issue and do something that symbolizes having it out of your life (burning it, burying it, throwing it away, and so on).
10. To recover from a traumatic event or to prevent problems, you can also develop stability and connective rituals: regularly repeated activities that help connect you to yourself or to others and help life feel stable and predictable for you and others.

The Ten Commandments for Parents or, Beware of Experts

> There are three rules for writing the novel. Unfortunately, no one knows what they are.
>
> —Somerset Maugham

There was once a man who gave a class for parents. He called it "Ten Commandments for Parents." Parents, being insecure about their abilities, came from far and near to attend his class and learn how to be better parents. At this time the man was not married and had no children. One day he met the woman of his dreams, and eventually they got married. In time they had a child. He then retitled his class, "Five Suggestions for Parents." In time they were blessed with another child. He then renamed the class, "Three Tentative Hints for Parents." After their third child was born, he stopped teaching the class altogether.

Whenever I write a book, I am painfully aware that life is more complex than anything even the wisest and best-written book can contain. So I hope you take this book in the spirit in which it was intended. Take anything that is helpful and disregard anything that doesn't work or that you feel invalidates you or doesn't fit with your values or who you are. I am reminded of what Mark Twain once wrote: "Be careful about reading health books. You may die of a misprint." Trust yourself and pay attention to what works for you. If you are in therapy or are following some teacher or leader and what you are doing is not working, don't keep doing that. Use your common sense. Even the material in this book should be suspect. If it doesn't work, don't use it—using it would be insanity. So, think of the ideas in this book as being like those three tentative hints. (I haven't stopped writing or teaching yet.) They are helpful only if they produce a result in your life. Otherwise, they are just good ideas.

TAKE ACTION AND ATTEND TO WHAT WORKS

Figure out what sucks, then don't do *that*!

—Agency.com unofficial motto

The essence of the solution-oriented approach is a very pragmatic principle: If what you are doing is not working, do something different. Pay attention to the results you get when you change what you are doing. If it works, keep doing it. If it doesn't work, try something new again.

Someone described this approach as *ready, fire, aim* (as opposed to the usual ready, aim, fire). Prepare, try something, and then make adjustments until you get the results you intended.

What stops people from living this way much of the time? They keep doing the same thing over and over, expecting that they will get different results. Their ideas and habits keep them in the same restricted path, like the polar bear at the zoo who was tethered when first placed in his enclosure, since it wasn't finished and there was the danger that he might escape. After the enclosure was completed, he was freed of the tether, but he continued to pace in the same restricted area.

Similarly, we sometimes do ineffective things over and over again, and view things the same way over and over again, and therefore stay stuck where we don't want to be (and don't have to be, I might add). We simply don't see that there are other possibilities. In this book, I have provided a menu of possibilities for changing these painfully ineffective patterns.

There is a story about America's quest to put a man on the moon. When President John F. Kennedy first announced this goal in a speech to the American public, many people were excited about it and committed to making J.F.K.'s vision a reality. Soon after the initial excitement, however, the naysayers came out in force. "That goal is impossible," they declared, "because we haven't got a metal alloy that will withstand the heat of reentry into the earth's atmosphere." So the people who were committed to realizing the goal got busy and, after much effort, created such an alloy. Next, the naysayers said, "Okay, well you've got the alloy, but there is no way we have enough computing power in small enough packages to make the massive calculations we need in order to communicate on-the-fly course changes to the spaceship." So, the people who were committed to the goal got to work and soon produced the silicon chips that would give the kind of computing power needed for such a task. And on and on it went. The point is that the people who were committed to a future in which the United States put a man on the moon kept taking actions and changing how they were thinking about the situation until they found a solution. They had to acknowledge problems, but they also had to keep possibilities open and stay flexible.

Most self-help books and psychological theories are like those naysayers who don't believe that change is possible. On the other side, there are people who are so positive that they don't even acknowledge or recognize problems.

Solution-oriented therapy recognizes problems and barriers and keeps trying experiments until the desired results are obtained. In order to do this, it is important to both attend to results and focus on what works. In order to be solution oriented, you must be willing to make mistakes, to correct your actions to produce results, and to avoid the paralysis of perfectionism and always having to know why things are or aren't working. You can't be satisfied with merely having a good explanation of why you don't or can't get certain results. You can't be attached to your beliefs or stories about yourself or the world if they get in the way of changing the things you hope to change. And you can't even get too attached to a particular *way* of accomplishing the result. Stay open to new possibilities. When in a dilemma, do something different!

Summary of Solution Keys

Solution Key 1: **Break Problem Patterns**

Solution Key 2: **Find and Use Solution Patterns**

Solution Key 3: **Acknowledge Your Feelings and the Past Without Letting Them Determine Your Actions in the Present and the Future**

Solution Key 4: **Shift Your Attention**

Solution Key 5: **Imagine a Future that Leads Back to Solutions in the Present**

Solution Key 6: **Change Problem Stories into Solution Stories**

Solution Key 7: **Use Spirituality to Transcend or Resolve Problems**

Solution Key 8: **Use Action Talk to Solve Relationship Problems**

Solution Key 9: **Perform a Resolution Ritual to Resolve Unfinished Issues from the Past**

Solution Key 10: **Develop Stability and Connective Rituals to Prevent Problems and Create Connections**

SOLUTION-ORIENTED RESOURCES

Books, Tapes, and Other Resources You Might Find Helpful

A Woman's Guide to Changing Her Man (Without His Even Knowing) by Michele Weiner-Davis (Golden Books, 1998). This is Michele's latest. The title is self-explanatory. This is available as an audiotape as well.

Change Your Life and Everyone in It by Michele Weiner-Davis (published by Fireside, 1996). This was called *Fire Your Shrink* when it was first published in hardcover. It is a guide to solving your own problems without therapy using the solution-oriented approach. It is available as an audiotape as well.

Counseling Toward Solutions by Linda Metcalf (Simon & Schuster/Center for Applied Research in Education, 1995). This book applies the solution-oriented approach to schools and is primarily for teachers, school counselors, and principals, but it could be used by anyone who has or works with children.

Divorce Busting by Michele Weiner-Davis (Fireside, 1993). This is Michele's first book for the general public. It focuses on how couples or either partner can use the solution-oriented method to prevent divorce.

In Search of Solutions: A New Direction in Psychotherapy by William Hudson O'Hanlon and Michele Weiner-Davis (Norton, 1988). Michele and I worked out the basics of solution-oriented therapy, and this is our first book on the subject. It was written for therapists, so it may not be for you. But if you are a counselor or want a more theoretical understanding of this approach, this book may be useful. Michele and I both have gone on to write books, like the one you are reading, that are geared more to the general reading audience, because we are so excited about getting the word out about this effective new approach to solving problems.

Parenting Toward Solutions by Linda Metcalf (Prentice-Hall, 1996). This book teaches parents how to use the solution-oriented approach with their children to both solve and prevent problems.

Stop Blaming, Start Loving (in hardcover: *Love Is a Verb*) by Bill O'Hanlon and Pat Hudson (Norton, 1996). This is a book in which my coauthor and I focus on applying the solution-oriented approach to relationships.

Bill O'Hanlon offers seminars and consultation to groups and businesses. Contact him through Possibilities, 551 Cordova Road, Suite 715, Santa Fe, NM 87501; 800-381-2374; email: PossiBill@aol.com; website: http://www.doonethingdifferent.com.

REFERENCES

Kaminer, W. (1993). *I'm dysfunctional, you're dysfunctional: The recovery movement and other self-help fashions.* New York: Vintage Books.

Lederer, W. J. and Jackson, Don D. (1990). *The mirages of marriage.* New York: W.W. Norton & Company.

Lord, B. B. (1991). *Legacies: A Chinese mosaic.* New York: Fawcett Books.

Rouse, J. (1985, October). "Commencement Address," *Johns Hopkins Magazine*, p. 12.

INDEX